ILLUSTRATED BY

COLOURED REPRESENTATIONS

OF THE

NATURAL AND ARTIFICIAL INSECT.

AND ACCOMPANIED BY

A few Observations and Instructions

RELATIVE TO

TROUT-AND-GRAYLING FISHING.

BY ALFRED RONALDS.

Second Edition.

WITH TWENTY COPPER PLATES

"Devouring Ephemerals! Can you not suffer the poor insects to sport out their day? They must be insipid eating—but here are some savoury exceedingly * * * * * * they carry *sauce piquante* in their tails. Do try the taste of this Bobber—but any of the three you please—There! Hold fast Kirby—for that's a Whopper."

CHRISTOPHER NORTH

LONDON:

LONGMAN, ORME, BROWN, GREEN,
AND LONGMANS.

1839.

PREFACE

TO THE FIRST EDITION.

The Author of this little work entreats that it may be considered and judged of as the labour, or rather the amusement of an amateur; whose chief object has been to facilitate to the Tyro in the art, the making and choice of artificial flies, on a plan of elucidation derived from personal experience.

Having himself sorely felt the inadequacy of mere verbal instructions to enable him to imitate the natural fly correctly, or even approximatively, and the little utility of graphical illustrations unaccompanied by the principal requisite, viz. colour, he has been induced to paint both the natural and artificial fly from nature, to etch them with his own hand, and to colour, or superintend the colouring of each particular impression.

He therefore presumes to hope that he

has succeeded in giving a useful collection of the leading flies for every month in the season, and that any one, who may be led by it to a choice of flies from the stock of the manufacturer, or to the construction of his own, will not have cause to repent of having consulted the catalogue, chiefly composing the fourth Chapter.

But since in his endeavours to improve the art of fly-making, careful observations were made relative to some of the habits of the Trout and Grayling, and of many insects upon which these fish prey; it is hoped that a few of these observations, intermixed with a little useful information, and some remarks on other points more or less connected with the principal subject, will not be thought inappropriate. These form the subjects of the three preceding Chapters.

Chiswick, June, 1836.

PREFACE

TO THE SECOND EDITION.

The favourable judgement passed upon these humble labours, by the respectable Magazines and Journals, which have condescended to review them, the promptitude with which indulgent brother anglers have responded to that decision, and the very encouraging terms in which it was pronounced, have constituted the natural and pleasing motives for printing this second edition.

A correction (concerning the weight of Trouts, usually rising to a fly,) with which the learned and tasteful Christopher North seasons *his* most grateful dish of praise, is adopted on the occasion, with profound reverence, by one, who, although not ranking amongst the *elite* of Scottish Anglers, ever rejoices in doing fealty and honour to the great and glorious modern Sire of *every* true born British Angler.*

To a friend in need and *in deed*, C. S. Hall, Esq., his sincere acknowledgment of deep obligation for timely and efficient support, must also be specially expressed; and from an experienced sportsman, his judicious reviewer, in the New Sporting Magazine, he cannot (however irregular the proceeding may be) withhold his hearty thanks.

He also avails himself of the opportunity to publicly apologize for not having adequately met some of the earlier demands for

---

* Vide Blackwood's Edin. Mag. June, 1838; New Monthly Mag. Aug. 1836; New Sporting Mag. Sept. and Oct. 1836; Examiner, Sept. 26th, 1836; Atlas, Aug. 13th, 1836; Literary Gazette, July 15th 1836; Staffordshire Advertiser, Aug. 13th and 20th, 1836, and June 9th, 1838.

The view to interests near at home, which is (avowedly) mixed up with a higher motive in citing these valuable authorities, will perhaps be deemed excusable, seeing that a fry of "*odd little fish*" (which the consummate eloquence of the great Christopher himself could never induce to devour a single Green Dragon, either alive, sauced, or painted), must nevertheless be supplied with *something* to rise at every day, and trained, *at least*, to distinguish the Little-dark-spinner from the Great-dark-drone.

copies. The insufficiency partly arose from a strong determination to spare no pains upon the colouring of the flies and palmers; but he begs leave to assure his future patrons, that, although practice has now enabled him to maintain an ample stock of paintings, it has not impaired that resolve in the smallest degree. Indeed a new incentive to exertion arises from the recent appearance of other works on angling, which, valuable as they may be in many respects, are not, in his *partial* opinion, at all calculated to satisfy the *chief* wants and wishes of the accomplished flyfisher; *coloured* flies and palmers being wholly *omitted* in them.

This edition results from a careful revision of the former, and comprehends several improvements, amongst which may be reckoned greater exactness in the delineation of certain hooks, and the addition of a frontispiece.

The two little foot notes at pp. 14 and 16, are mere indices to some good remarks and experiments relative to the *iris* colours of, and to the sense of taste in, fish, &c.

and are intended for the use of such curious Anglers as may not happen to have considered these subjects in the light in which they are there presented. Wider discussions might soon have become incompatible with our wish to avoid the error (not wholly avoided even in these manuals) of speaking too much of, to, or for, one's vain self.

Chiswick, June, 1839.

CONTENTS.

CHAPTER I.

OBSERVATIONS ON THE TROUT AND GRAYLING.

CHAPTER II.

OF TACKLE.

CHAPTER III.

MANNER OF FISHING FOR TROUT AND GRAYLING.

CHAPTER IV.

OF A SELECTION OF INSECTS, AND THEIR IMITATIONS, USED IN FLY FISHING.

THE

FLY-FISHERS ENTOMOLOGY.

Chapter I.

OBSERVATIONS ON THE TROUT AND GRAYLING.

Of the Trout. Measurement, Weight, Fins, Colour, Condition, Haunts, &c. Description of a Fishing-hut or Observatory. The Trout's sense of Hearing. Sight. Taste and Smell. Manner of feeding, &c. Form, Weight, Fins, &c. of the Grayling. Colour. Condition. Haunts. Food.

Of the Trout there are several species or varieties described by Naturalists and Anglers, but the observations which follow are chiefly applicable to the Salmo Fario, or common Trout.

This much esteemed fish, when in the best condition, generally measures from the nose to the fork of the tail twice as much as the girth. The weight of those *usually* taken with the fly is from two ounces to two pounds and a half, and of those *sometimes* taken from four to five pounds, but all under three or four ounces are too small for the creel.

He has eight fins (viz.) one dorsal, one anal,

one caudal, two pectoral, two ventral, and a little fleshy one without spines on the back near the tail-fin.

Sir H. Davy says (Salmonia, p. 73.) " I have known the number of spines in the Pectoral fins different in different varieties of Trout; I have seen them twelve, thirteen, and fourteen: but the anal fin always, I believe, contains eleven spines, the dorsal twelve or thirteen, the ventral nine, and the caudal twenty-one."

The back fin has a pale brown colour, with darker brown spots upon it; the others (including the tail) have a red tint. The colour of the back when in perfect condition, (which is generally in May, or in some waters not until June), is, usually, a dark olive green, studded with a mixture of black and brownish spots. The sides are shaded off from the olive to a greenish yellow, studded with red spots; the black spots gradually vanishing. Lower down the yellow tint approaches a salmon colour, and the belly is nearly white, without any spots.

The whole surface of the fish, when in good condition, always presents a beautiful gradation of tints: but his complexion varies greatly in different waters, and also in all waters at different periods of the year. It is principally modified by his state of health.

Sir H. Davy says: "The colouring matter is not in the scales, but in the surface of the skin immediately beneath them, and is probably a secretion easily affected by the health of the animal." (Salmonia, p. 40.)

After spawning time (i. e.) the month of October or November, both the male and female lose their more beautiful tints, become thinner, and are considered quite out of season; and towards the end of the winter, and even in March, some little insects, like leaches, about an inch long, called water lice, are found adhering to them; when in this sad state the cooked flesh cuts soft, and looks white, (very different from the rich salmon colour, which always indicates good condition). Every true disciple of Izaak Walton who may take such a thin *black looking* Trout will return the lanky trophy to its native element.

Haunts.

To enumerate the rivers, streams, and brooks of this country, which the common Trout inhabits, would be an endless, and useless task; he may be said to frequent almost all of them, and will even sometimes be discovered in a mere ditch (in spawning time) having scarcely depth of water enough to cover the back.

He delights in rapid clear-running waters, with

a rocky or gravelly bottom. An attempt has been made in the annexed plan to point out his favourite haunts, &c. in such waters. They are the tail of a stream, (i. e.) the end of a little rapid, or swifter running portion of the current, as A, the junction of little rapids formed by water passing round an obstruction in the midst of the general current, as B, and such tracts as C, where a chain of bubbles or little floating objects indicate the course of the principal current; which course is chiefly dependent upon various reflections of the water, from projecting banks, rocks, scours, and shoals, and may often be guessed at, when not sufficiently visible, by attending to the position of the banks, &c. At roots of trees, or in other places where the froth (called in Staffordshire Beggar's Balm) collects, and in little whirlpools, as G, and eddies he will often be found. All such places are by far the most favourable for sport; for insects follow the same course as the bubbles, &c. and are sought there by the fish.

The larger Trout are on the scours, as at D, in the night, chasing minnows and other small fish. In the day, they are cautiously watching for food in deep holes, under hollow banks, or roots of trees, or in the angles of rocks, as E. In May and June, when the fish are strong, they are also to be found in the more rapid parts of the water, as F.

Pl I

These remarks, although not strictly applicable to the Trout of all streams, may still, perhaps, not be found useless, in a great variety of instances, particularly in respect of brooks.

His great shyness renders it extremely difficult to obtain any accurate knowledge of his habits, by ocular demonstration. Even a thick bush will seldom be found sufficiently opaque to conceal the observer.

Observatory.

With a view to obviate this difficulty I built a little fishing Hut, or Observatory, of heath, overhanging a part of the river Blythe, near Uttoxeter, in Staffordshire, which seemed favourable for the purpose. Its form was octagonal, and it had three windows, which being situated only four feet and a half above the surface of the water, allowed a very close view of it. The middle one commanded a scour, each of the two others a small whirlpool or eddy. The curtains of the windows were provided with peepholes, so that the fish could not see his observer, and a bank was thrown up, in order to prevent a person approaching the entrance of the hut from alarming the fish.

The stream was regularly fished, and nothing else was done to interfere with the natural state of the animal.

The stationary position in which he is enabled

to maintain himself in the most rapid stream, poised as it were like a hawk in the air, was the first thing which seemed worth noting at this fishing-hut. Even the tail, which is known to be the principal organ of propulsion, can scarcely be observed to move, and the fins, which are used to balance the fish, seem quite useless, except when he sees an insect; then he will dart with the greatest velocity through the opposing current at his prey, and quickly return. The station which he occupies in this manner is invariably well chosen. Should a favourite haunt where food is concentrated by the current be rather crowded by his fellows, he will prefer contending with them for a share of it, to residing long in an unfruitful situation.

A Trout will chiefly frequent one place during all the summer months. It is well known that he quits the larger waters, and ascends the smaller brooks for the purpose of spawning in October and November, when the male assists the female in making a hole in the gravel wherein to deposit the ovæ. By some it is supposed, that they both lie dormant in the mud during the greatest severity of the winter.

Sense of Hearing.

In order that we might be enabled to ascertain the truth of a common assertion (viz.) that fish can hear voices in conversation on the banks of a stream, my friend, the Rev. Mr. Brown, of Gratwich, and myself, selected for close observation a Trout poised about six inches deep in the water, whilst a third gentleman, who was situated behind the fishing-house, (i. e.) diametrically opposite to the side where the fish was, fired off one barrel of his gun. The possibility of the flash being seen by the fish was thus wholly prevented, and the report produced not the slightest apparent effect upon him.

The second barrel was then fired; still he remained immovable; evincing not the slightest symptom of having heard the report. This experiment was afterwards often repeated, and precisely similar results were invariably obtained; neither could I, or other persons, ever awaken symptoms of alarm in the fishes near the hut by shouting to them in the loudest tones, although our distance from them did not sometimes exceed six feet. The experiments were not repeated so often as to habituate them to the sound.

It is possible that fishes may be in some manner affected by vibrations communicated to their element, either directly, or by the intervention of aerial pulsations; although it does not seem to be clearly proved that they possess any organ appropriated exclusively to the purpose of hearing. At all events it appears, that neither the above mentioned explosions, nor the loud voices, had power to produce vibrations in the water, which could so affect them.

Leaving the discussion of this intricate subject to more able and learned speculators, it is sufficient to know that the above mentioned Trout had no ears to hear either the voices or the gun; and I firmly believe, that the zest which friendly chat often imparts to the exercise of our captivating art, need never be marred by an apprehension that sport will be impaired thereby.

Sight.

Of all the senses in fish, sight is perhaps the one of most importance to them. Their eyes are perfectly adapted to the element they inhabit; indeed their subsistence seems to depend mainly upon the great sensibility of the optic nerve and the just adaptation of the crystalline and other humours to their proper office.

A fish can perhaps frequently distinguish (with greater or less distinctness) much *more* of objects which are out of his own element than it is often imagined that he can.

When A B (fig. 1. plate 2), for instance, situated upon a certain eminence at a given distance from a fish, C, which is near the bottom of the water,

Fig 1

looks over the edge of a bank, D, in the direction A F Z, he might (if unacquainted with the laws of refraction) imagine, that neither the fish C, nor any other fish below the line of his direct vision, AFZ, could see him; whereas C could see A B by means of the pencil of light, A F C E B, *bent*, or refracted at the surface of the water, E F, and the image of A B would appear in the eye of the fish shortened and transferred to G H. The fish in fact could see the whole of the man, round, or over the corner of the bank, by the aid of the water above C, if both were situated as respectively represented in the diagram; but if the surface of the water should be at I K, (i. e.) about as low as the fishes' eye, then, he could not see any part of the figure A B, because a straight or unrefracted pencil of light, A C B, would be obstructed by the bank.

Increments of obliquity in pencils of light falling upon a surface of water, &c. are accompanied by increments of refraction, not in *direct* ratio to the increase of obliquity, but in a much higher ratio; and indistinctness of vision in an eye receiving the pencil increases, *on this account*, in some similar high ratio.

The bending or refraction which a pencil of light, as N E O F M, (fig. 2), falling very obliquely upon the surface of the water, undergoes before arriving at the eye of a fish, as at O, is sufficient to produce very great indistinctness and distortion of the image of M P formed in his eye.

(Perhaps indistinctness of vision may, *on other accounts*, take place in the eye of a fish looking through air. The crystalline and perhaps other humours may not be capable of such comprehensive adjustment as would enable him to see so distinctly through air as he can through water).

But long before a pencil of light, as N E L, becomes horizontal it will not enter the water at all; consequently, although the fish at O may see the upper part of the man situated at M P, he will do so very indistinctly, and in a new position, because the pencil NEOFM will be very much refracted; he will not see the part, N L, of the man at all, because the pencil, N E L, does not enter the water at all; and he will see probably his legs, L P, (in the clear water), because there is neither refraction nor obstruction to prevent him. So that the figure M P will, in the eye of the fish, be cut up into two portions separated from each other by a long unsubstantial interval. The application of these two little theorems to the use of the fisherman is too obvious to need pointing out here.*

---

* This diagram is constructed on two well-known optical laws, viz. first, the sine a. b. of the angle of incidence, A E f, of a ray of light passing out of air into water, is always to the sine, c. d, of the angle of refraction, C E e, as about four to three: and, secondly, light will

Taste and Smell.

It seemed almost impossible to devise experiments relative to the sense of smell in fishes, which would offer the prospect of satisfactory results, without depriving the animal of sight; the cruelty of which operation deterred me from prosecuting the enquiry.

Observations on the taste of fishes are involved in still greater difficulty. I once threw upon the water, from my hut (by blowing them through a tin tube) successively, ten dead house-flies, towards a Trout known to me by a white mark upon the nose, (occasioned by the wound of a hook), all of which he took. Thirty more, with *Cayenne pepper and mustard* plastered on the least conspicuous parts of them, were then administered in the same manner. These he also seized; twenty of them at the instant they touched the water, and allowing no time for the dressing to be dispersed; but the other ten remained a second or two upon the surface before he swallowed them, and a small portion of the dressing parted and sank. The next morning several exactly similar doses were taken by the same fish, who was appa-

---

not pass out of air into water, if the angle of incidence, N E f, (fig. 2), exceeds about 88 degrees (but will be reflected).

The old experiment of the shilling and the basin of water affords an easy practical demonstration of the first mentioned theorem.

rently so well contented with the previous day's treatment that he seemed to enjoy them heartily. From these and similar experiments, such as Trout taking flies dipped in honey, oil, vinegar, &c. I concluded that if the animal has taste his palate is not peculiarly sensitive.

My experience goes to prove contrary to the opinion of some who say that the Trout will take *every* insect, that he does not feed upon the hive Bee, or Wasp, and that he very rarely takes the Humble Bee.

It seemed to be a common practice with those who plied for food near the hut, to lay an embargo upon almost every little object which floated down the stream, taking it into the mouth, sometimes with avidity, sometimes more slowly, or cautiously, as if to ascertain its fitness, or unfitness, for food, and frequently to reject it instantly.* This seems to favour the notion that if the Trout has not a taste similar to our own he may be endowed with some equivalent species of sensation. It may also account for his taking a *nondescript* artificial fly, but it furnishes no plea to quacks and bunglers, who, inventing or espousing a new theory, whereby to hide their want of skill or spare their pains, would kill all the fish with one fly, as some doctors would

* They might possibly have appropriated some little insect embarked

cure all diseases by one pill. If a Trout rejects the *brown* hive Bee at the time that he greedily swallows the March-*brown* fly, it is clear that the imitation should be as exact as possible of the last, and as dissimilar as possible to the first.

I have very frequently watched fish in an apparently hesitating attitude when Bees and Wasps were within their ken. How far either smell or taste may be concerned in this seeming indecision I cannot determine.

On one occasion I observed an Humble Bee which floated down the stream visited by a Trout, who suffered himself to descend also with the current just under the bee, his nose almost touching it for about three feet, but he struck away without taking it.

At another time I saw a fish swim up to an Humble Bee which was thrown to him, and examine it very attentively, he then cautiously and leisurely took it in his mouth and descended with it, but immediately afterwards gave it up; he then seemed to be closely occupied with another Humble Bee swimming up to and away from it six times, each time almost touching it with his nose. Ultimately he took this also, but immediately rejected it.

Sir H. Davy (Salmonia, page 28) says, "The principal use of the nostrils in fishes, I believe, is to assist in the propulsion of water through the gills for performing the office of respiration; but I think there are some nerves in these organs which give fishes a sense of the qualities of water, or of substances dissolved in or diffused through it similar to our sense of smell or perhaps rather our sense of taste, for there can be no doubt that fishes are attracted by scented worms which are sometimes used by anglers that employ ground baits." Also page 184, he says, "We cannot judge of the senses of animals that breathe water—that separate air from water by their gills; but it seems probable that as the quality of the water is connected with their life and health, they must be exquisitely sensible to changes in water, and must have similar relations to it, that an animal with the most delicate nasal organs has to the air."

Surely no reasoning can be more sound than this. Should not our endeavours be directed, rather to the discovery of senses in fish, which we have not, than to attempts at comparison between our own senses and theirs?*

Having examined the stomachs of many Trouts taken in almost every week throughout the three last entire fishing seasons, with a view chiefly to assist my choice of flies for the catalogue below;

* Those who may have curiosity enough to pursue this interesting topic, might possibly find amusement in the perusal of a paper read to the French Institute by M. Duméril, August 24th, 1807, and translated in Nicholson's Journal, vol. xxix. p. 344, in which many circumstances judiciously adduced, and fairly reasoned on, lead him to three general

I found that his food consisted besides Flies and Caterpillars, of Larvæ, Squillæ (or fresh water Shrimps) small Fish, young Crawfish, Spiders, Millipedes, Earwigs, and the Water Beetle. I never discovered Frogs, Snails, or Mice, but have no doubt that other waters afford other fare even "*Sauces piquantes* of fish hooks."

A convenient method of examining the contents of the stomach is to put the materials into a hair sieve and pump clean water upon them; when parted and sufficiently clean the whole may be put into a large cup, *full of clean water*, for examination.

THE GRAYLING

Is a more elegantly formed fish than the Trout. He has a smaller head and mouth, is broader across the shoulders, and tapers off more rapidly to the tail, which is more forked. The front of the eye is elliptical, and the pupil much more elongated than that of the Trout, the side towards the nose being drawn out to an acute angle. The opposite side is less acute.

His back fin is very large. It has twenty-three

---

conclusions, viz.: 1st. That the organ of taste in fishes, if taste they have, "does not reside in the mouth." 2ndly. That the sensation of taste, or some equivalent sensation, "is imparted to them by the apparatus which had hitherto been considered as adapted to perceive the emanations of odorate bodies" And Lastly, "That no real smell can be perceived in water."

spines, the ventral fin (near the head) has sixteen, the pectoral ten, the anal fourteen, and the tail eighteen.

He sometimes grows to about three pounds in weight, though one of a pound and a half is considered a good sized fish, and larger are not very often caught with the fly, the usual weight being from two ounces to a pound of those which rise freely to it. The fish of the spawn of April or May (measuring from the nose to the fork of the tail) grows to about six inches by the next April.

A general tint which may be called a light blue silvery grey, pervades nearly the whole surface of his body, except the belly, which is white or nearly so, but the scales often exhibit by *deflected* light a great variety of colours dependant upon the positions chosen to view them from.* The

---

* From a very curious series of experiments detailed by Sir David Brewster in his Treatise on Optics, (p. 113 et seq.) "it is obvious that the splendid colours of mother of pearl, &c. are produced by a particular configuration of surface, and by examining this surface with microscopes, he discovered in almost every specimen a grooved structure like the delicate texture of the skin at the top of an infant's finger," &c. By cutting grooves upon steel at the distance of from the 2,000th to the 10,000th of an inch apart, Mr. Barton produced still more brilliant hues, and his *iris* ornaments on brass and other metal, buttons, and articles of female embellishment, are the result of machinery constructed on this grooving principle, upon which, we believe, depends the above mentioned and many similar phenomena (as in the peacock's feather, &c.) In sun, gas, or candle-light some iris ornaments rival "the brilliant flashes of the diamond." (A superb example of a grooved medallion may be seen in the library of the Royal Institution). But in day light and in ordinary circumstances the colours of the iris ornaments are not easily distinguished.

back and head are of a much darker grey, but its components cannot, perhaps, be particularized. Some lines of brown are intermixed with the grey of the sides, and a few black spots are seen near the shoulder. The back fin has a purplish tint studded with large dark spots, the other fins are not so red as those of the Trout, but have more yellow-brown in them shaded off with purple. The tail is a kind of slate colour. The colours vary a little in different waters, and, unlike the Trout, the better the condition, the *darker* is the fish, especially upon the back and head, "and you are to note," that the throat has a long very dark brown patch upon it, visible when the mouth is open, when he is in high condition, but it is hardly to be seen when he is out of order. He is, however, seldom or never found in the miserable state so common to Salmon and Trout after spawning.

The Grayling is an excellent fish both for sport and the table, and as his finest condition subsists during the Autumn and Winter months, when the Trout season ceases, the Angler finds great pleasure and consolation in visiting the streams in the autumn in search of him, or even on fine days in winter. On this account, those who have not the Grayling in their waters, would perhaps sometimes do well to try to introduce him.

The waters in which he thrives may be either

clear or discoloured, but a rather peculiar formation of the bed of the current seems to be required, his favourite streams having now somewhat shallow and rapid, then long, slow-running, deep, tracts; in which latter places he poises himself about three or four feet below the chain of insects, &c. as at H H (see plate 1.)

As he feeds principally on Larvæ and flies, he should, according to Malthus, be populous, (all other things being equal), in proportion as these insects are so.

Temperature, both atmospheric and aqueous, no doubt affects both the food and fish, as also may the chemical properties of the stratum over which the stream flows; the mineral held in solution by the fluid (which he breathes) cannot fail to affect his constitution in some measure.

But there exists no authority for the localities of the Grayling at all comparable with Sir H. Davy, who " has fished much in, and enquired much respecting the places where it is found." At p. 221 (Salmonia) he says, " In the Test, where the Grayling has been only recently introduced, they have sometimes been caught between three and four pounds; in this river I never took one above two pounds, but I have heard of one being taken of two pounds and a half. The Grayling is a rare fish in England, and has never been found in Scotland or Ireland; and there are few rivers containing all the conditions necessary for their increase. I know of no Grayling river farther West than the Avon, in Hampshire; they are found in some of the tributary streams of this river which rise in Wiltshire. I know of no river containing them on the North coast West of the Severn; there are very few only in the upper part of this river, and in the streams which form it in North Wales. There are a few in the Wye and its tributary streams. In the Lug, which flows through the next valley, in Herefordshire, many Grayling are found. In the Dee, as I said before, they are found, but are not common. In Derbyshire and Staffordshire, the Dove, the Wye, the Trent, and the Blythe, afford Grayling; in Yorkshire, on the North coast, some of the tributary streams of the Ribble,—and in the South, the Ure, the Wharfe, the Humber, the Derwent, and the streams that form it, particularly the Rye."

Again at page 203, he says, "Having travelled with the fishing-rod in my hand through most of the Alpine valleys in the South and East of Europe, and some of those in Norway and Sweden, I have always found the Char in the coldest and highest waters; the Trout in the brooks rising in the highest and coldest mountains; and the Grayling always lower where the temperature was milder: and if in hot countries, only at the foot of mountains, not far from sources which had the mean temperature of the atmosphere; as in the Vipacco, near Coritzea, and in the streams which gush forth from the limestone caverns of the Noric Alps.

"Besides temperature, Grayling require a peculiar character in the disposition of the water of rivers. They do not dwell like Trout in rapid shallow torrents; nor like Char or Chub in deep pools or lakes. They require a combination of stream and pool; they like a deep and still pool for rest, and a rapid stream above, and gradually declining shallow below, and a bottom where marl and loam is mixed with gravel; and they are not found abundant except in rivers that have these characters."

The Rev. Mr. Low. says, (p. .), "The Grayling is frequent in the Orkney Islands, as it is in Lapland and Switzerland; but it is rare in Scotland, and confined in England to the Avon near Salisbury, the Ure near Fountain's Abbey, the Dee between Corwan and Bala, and the Dove; also the Trent, the Wharfe, the Humber, the Rye, and the Derwent."

The Grayling is seldom known to take the Minnow, and I have never found any in his stomach, although I have taken out much Larvæ covered with cases of sand, and some having six stones attached to each, as also Larvæ when in the mummy state. I have always found flies, and those principally of the more delicate sorts of Ephemeræ.

He rises with great velocity and almost perpendicularly to seize his prey, at the top of the water, and descends as quickly after making a summerset, for the performance of which feat, the figure of his body and the great dorsal fin, seem well adapted; his agility on this occasion is indeed so great, that he seems a phantom or flitting shadow; hence, say some, his name *Umbra* corrupted to *Umber*. It has been supposed that he feeds upon the water-thyme, but I never found any vegetable whatever in the stomach, though I have opened as many Grayling as Trout. He has, however, a rather peculiar scent when just taken from the water, fragrant and grateful to the fisherman, and thought by many to resemble that of thyme, consequently has been also called (by Linnæus) the Salmo Thymallus, and by St. Ambrose "the flower of fishes."

He seems to congregate more than the Trout, and is not so easily driven from his station by an approach, but whether this be owing to his lying lower down in the water, or from his being naturally a less timid fish, remains yet to be ascertained.

Chapter II.

OF TACKLE, ETC.

Rod. Line. Reel. Foot Line. Hook. Dubbing Bag. General Directions for making a Fly and a Palmer. Fly Books and Boxes. Creel. Landing Net, et ceteras. Dyes for Feathers.

Like the bow of the Archer, the Rod of the Angler should be duly proportioned in dimensions and weight, to the strength and stature of him who wields it. The strong or tall man, may venture upon a rod about fourteen or fifteen feet long: but to the person who is shorter or less robust, one so short even as twelve or twelve feet and a half, and light in proportion, is recommended, as the command will be sooner obtained, and with very much less fatigue to the arm. The best materials are, ash for the stock, lancewood for the middle, and bamboo for the top; the but should have a hole drilled down it with a spare top in it, and a spike is made to screw into the end, which will be found useful to stick into the ground, and keep the rod upright, when landing a good fish. The ferrules of brass should fit into each other with screws.

A good Rod should be such that its pliability may be felt in the hand, yet it should not deviate or droop by its own weight, if held by the but in a horizontal position, more than three or four inches from a straight line.

The rings are usually too small; not allowing such slight obstacles on the line, as can never be totally prevented, to run with sufficient freedom through them; they should all be of the size of those usually put upon the stock. The rod may not have quite so neat an appearance thus treated, but this will be found to be amply compensated in its use; for the sudden stops occasioned by an accident to the line, whilst being pulled up rapidly, has often caused the loss of a good fish, the straining of, if not breaking, a good rod, and sometimes a breach of the third commandment.

Rings may be had (slit down the middle) in the manner of key rings, very little heavier, yet larger than the usual rings. These can be easily substituted upon the little metallic loops in lieu of the smaller rings, by the possessor of a rod himself, without at all injuring it.

Line.

The beginner should not take the finest Fly Line he can buy, but rather choose the strongest line of this kind to be had, since too fine a line will not only be more likely to break than a heavier one, but will not be so easy for him to throw.

Reel.

Notwithstanding the many complaints which have been made of the Reel usually sold, no very great improvement upon it seems to have been put into practice. The principal requisites seem to be, first, a capability of winding up the line rapidly ; secondly, smallness ; thirdly, lightness ; fourthly, freedom from liability to derangement.

Perhaps rather too much of the first requisite is generally sacrificed, for the sake of cheapness, and for the purpose of obtaining the second and third. A reel having a *sheave* upon which the line is to be wound, whose groove for the reception of the line is three quarters of an inch broad, whose barrel is two inches in diameter, and whose total diameter is two inches and three quarters, would receive a trout-line of twenty yards perfectly well. The whole diameter of such a reel need not exceed three inches and a quarter, nor the whole breadth one inch and a quarter. The wheels might multiply five times, and therefore the *average rate* at which it would wind up the line would be nearly three feet for every revolution of the handle, whereas a common reel (now before me), multiplying four times, winds up at every turn of the handle, when the line is nearly out, only three inches, and when it is nearly wound up, eighteen inches, making a mean of ten inches and a half. The proposed reel would therefore wind up the line more than three times as fast, and besides this superior rapidity, would possess the advantage of winding up the line almost as quickly when it is nearly all out, as when it is nearly all in. It might also be so constructed as to weigh *very little* more than the common reel, made for such a line, and would be less liable to derangement, (which last advantage would be a consequence of both the multiplying wheels being larger than usual.)

A simple reel with a sheave of large diameter has been made of wood, and without multiplying wheels, but it has a very clumsy appearance, and is liable to obvious objections.

A reel has been invented lately containing a spiral spring which acts (in the manner of the spring in a window blind) upon the axis to wind up the line.

And it has been recently, and very ingeniously proposed by an experienced brother of our art, to inclose, either wholly or partially, a kind of reel in the but of the rod. If sufficient rapidity can be given to such a reel, without much liability to derangement (which does not seem a very difficult task), it will be an invaluable and elegant acquisition. This hint seems to have been *partially* adopted since the first edition appeared.

Bottom Line.

For making a good Bottom, or foot line, or casting line, gut is recommended in preference to weed, or hair; it should be of the very best quality, round, and of even thickness, clear, and white. By adopting the precautions recommended in the following instructions, it may be used fine, although as strong or nearly so as the end of the line. The length of the bottom should be about equal to that of the rod.

Four or five of the very finest lengths of gut should first be chosen, then three or four more of the middle size, and lastly one or two much stronger.

These must all be proved before they are put together, thus:—One end of a length must be put between the teeth, and the other pulled until the gut breaks at the weakest part. This operation must be repeated continually with the best portions, until they snap with considerable resistance. Then the ends may be reversed and the operation proceeded with as before, until the last remaining piece is deemed strong enough for its office. This manner of getting rid of the bad portions will not appear extravagant, but the contrary, when it is considered that the loss of a whole or large part of the foot-line, with a fly or two, and perhaps a fine Trout, may be the consequence of an undue weakness existing in any particular part of it.

These well-proved lengths of gut must now be lashed together with waxed silk, or tied by a knot, and the strongest must be provided with a large loop, whereby it may be attached to the line.

Hook.

The HOOK requires particular attention. It is sufficiently provoking to discover that one has made a good fly upon a bad hook; but to lose a good fish in consequence is truly awful.

The Kendal hook, see fig. 40, plate 17, is frequently preferred, if not made too long in the point. The Limerick is also a good hook for large flies, as at present made by O'Shaughnessy of Limerick, see fig. 29, plate 13. His is not too proud in the barb, and is generally properly tempered. The Carlisle hook may also rank amongst the good ones, fig. 38, plate 17. The Kirby is used by some.

To prove the temper of a hook, stick the point into a piece of soft wood before it is fastened to the gut and pull by the shank. If it is well tempered, it will not break or bend without considerable resistance.

Dubbing Bag.

The DUBBING BAG contains every thing in the world. Some people have very neat little cabinets made expressly; we cannot blame their taste, if they possess the organ of order.

Fly Making.

Many books, after trying to tell us how TO MAKE A FLY, very justly add, that the art cannot be told, it must be seen. We shall follow the fashion.

1. Take a piece of gut proved to be strong enough by the above mentioned process, and bite about a tenth of an inch at one extremity, so as to make it flat, (in order that it may be less liable to slip after being tied on to the hook). Then holding a fine thread well waxed with cobbler's wax, (A B C D, plate 3, fig. 1.) in one hand, whip a part of it three or four times round the end of the shank of the hook, beginning to whip at B, and leaving a few inches of thread at A B hanging down, with a pair of forceps, or little weight at the end of it.

2. Hold the bitten end E (fig. 2.) of the gut E C F, in contact with the shank of the hook, and wind tightly the portion of thread C D of fig. 1. first, once or twice round the gut close to the end of the shank, fig. 2. and then over the portion of gut C E, the three or four coils B C, already made, and the shank of the hook, C B E, leaving out the piece of thread A B, still hanging down.

3. Bring two or three stylish whisks from a red hackle into the position shewn in figure 3, and bind them securely there, for the tail, by means of the same end (c, d) of silk as was last used. Bind in, at the same time, the extremity of a piece of fine gold twist (e, f), and also an end of

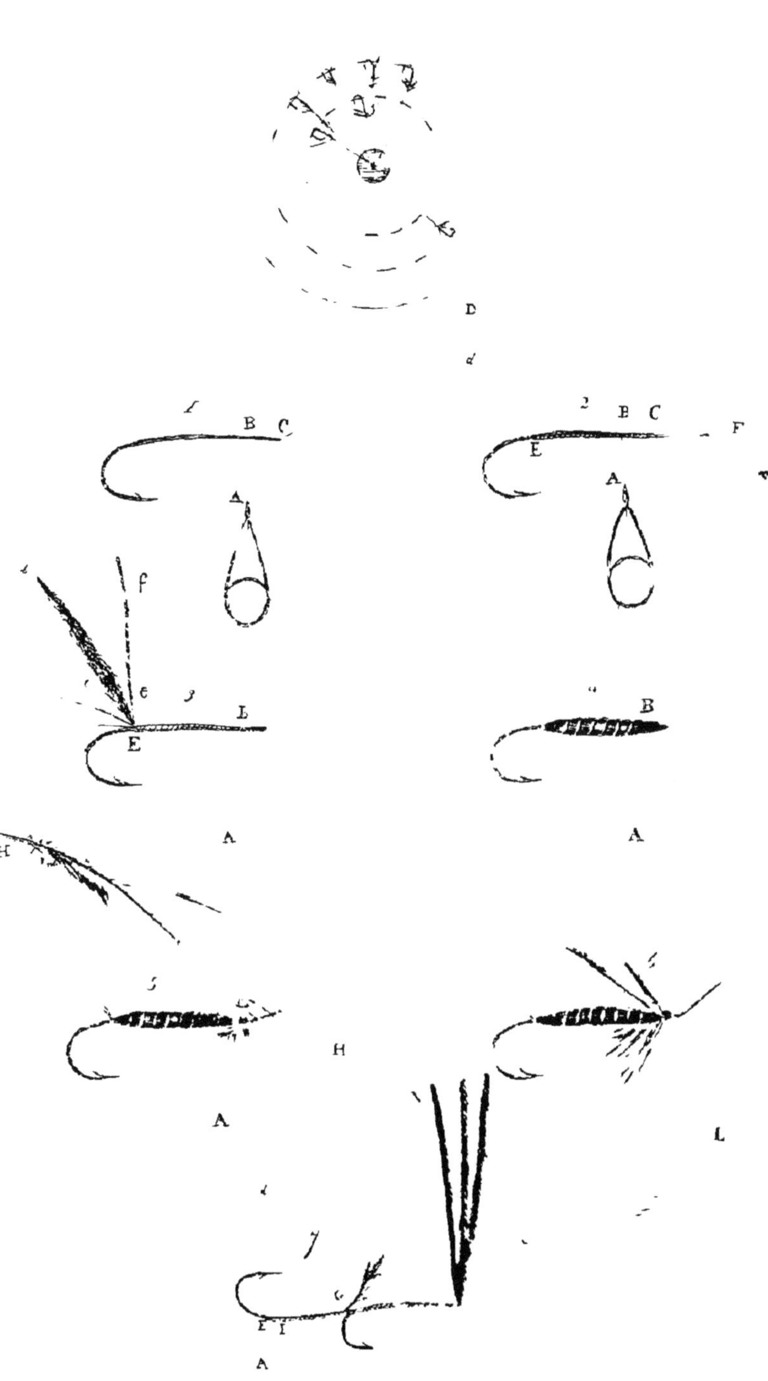
D
B C
B C
E
F
A
A
E
B
A
A
H
H
A
L
E I
A

some dubbing of orange and red floss silk mixed. Then spin the floss silk on to the remnant (c, d) of silk thread, and wind it on the shank, or wind it on the shank without spinning.

4. Warp the remnant (c, d) round the shank, &c. back to B, and make it fast there with the thread A B; then coil or rib the gold twist (e, f) over the coils made by c, d in the manner shewn in fig. 4, and make it fast also with the thread A B. This completes the body.

5. Bring the upper end of a red hackle stained amber colour into the position shewn in fig. 5, tie it there by means of the well waxed thread, A B, and cut off the projecting piece (G) of the hackle.

6. Wind the other part of the hackle, B H, (fig. 5) two or three times round the upper end of the body, and bind it tightly and neatly there (with A B), and in such manner that the fibres may stand as shewn in fig. 6. This represents legs.

7. Take two pieces, I K, fig. 6, from the under side of the wing of a starling, and bind them on (with the but ends towards the top of the shank) firmly and neatly, at nearly the same place B, (a little nearer to the top of the shank.) Part them, if you choose, snip off the but ends obliquely, bind the short stumps down upon the shank, &c. (so that they may not be seen) and

fasten off with the invisible knot of three coils.* You will now possess *a great red spinner* complete, provided always that you have seen a great deal more of the art than you have read, and that you have been yourself a tolerably good dubbing spinner.

To make a Buzz-fly with a hackle, (see fig. 5, plate 5) the upper or pointed end of the hackle must be tied at the tail E (fig. 3, plate 3) with the ends of the materials of the body (by means of the thread c, d) and the hackle must be wound up over the dubbing, and fastened off with the thread A B, after the gold or silver twist or other *ribbing* has been wound on and fastened off with A B.

If a Buzz-fly (as figs. 28 and 29, plate 13) is to be made with any other feather than a hackle, the feather should be stroked back, its pointed end should be tied on at the shoulder B, fig. 4, plate 3, of the fly, three or four coils of the feather should be made round the part above B, and the stands or fibres of the feather should be carefully picked out, as the coiling proceeds, otherwise it will not lie well. The but end of the feather must be tied in at the head of the fly with the thread A B, which must be fastened off as usual with the invisible knot of three coils.

---

* To make this knot: Make three loose coils over the fore finger of the left hand, pass the end of the thread under them, and draw each coil tight by pulling each separately as it were.

In making a fly with wings intended to represent natural wings at rest, (as fig. 2, plate 4), the hackle feather may, in some cases, be dispensed with, and a little of the dubbing may be left out in the warping, or picked out of the body with a needle, after the winding or warping, to serve for legs instead of the hackle feather. In every other respect the fly may be made in the manner prescribed for the great red Spinner. (See p. 28.)

When a hackle or other feather is used for the purpose of imitating a winged fly buzz, its tint should be lighter than that of the natural wings; for the effect of the buzzing motion is to give this lighter appearance.

To make a Palmer.

1. Bite the end of a strong piece of gut, and whip a part of the thread A B C D, fig. 1, plate 3, round the end of the shank of a hook (as before, see page 28).

2. Place the gut in contact with the hook, and wind the portion of thread, C D, of fig. 1, over the part of gut C E, fig. 2, the three or four coils B C, and the shank of the hook C B E, &c. *not* leaving the end of thread as before hanging from B, but including it in the new coils, and allowing it to hang from E (fig. 7).

3. Wind rapidly (or run) c d back again to C, and include the but end of a red hackle G H

(fig. 7) in the four or five last coils of this winding.

4. Bring another hook, I, into the position shewn in fig. 7, and attach it to the gut E C F; by winding the same thread, c d, round its shank and the gut. Then wind c d two or three times round the gut only (close to the end of the hook) and back again two or three coils over the shank, to form the head of the Palmer.

5. Tie in (with the same thread, c d) another hackle, K L, by the but, together with three peacock's hurls, M N.

6. Wind the thread c d with the peacock's hurls, spun or rather twisted on it, back to C, and make it fast there (or hold it tight), but do not cut off the remnant. Also wind the hackle K L over the dubbing of peacock's hurl back to C, and tie it, picking out any strands which may happen to be tied in, and snip off the ends of K L.

7. Now wind the remaining dubbing-spun piece of silk (c d) over the coils of thread and the shank of the first mentioned hook down to E, bind it there with the well-waxed thread A B; wind also the hackle G H over the dubbing down to E, make all fast by means of the thread A B and the invisible knot; snip off all the remnants, and your red Palmer (see fig. 45, page 19) will be ready to make a pilgrimage in search of a Trout.

Fly Books, Boxes, et cetera.

Having lost many flies out of the boxes and books usually sold, I at last adopted the following little device of a friend, which has certainly served to retain them better, and to keep them in better order for selection. Several round pieces of card-board, as fig. 8, plate 3, are first fitted to the box. At the centre of each of these is fixed a piece of cork, round which two concentric circles of stitches of gut (or sometimes very well waxed fine silk thread) are formed, and they are covered at the back (or under side of the card) with a piece of paper pasted over them. On the upper side and under these stitches the barbs of the hooks are passed, the long ends of the gut are put through a hole in the centre of the cork, and these cards are packed in the box over each other, without injury or derangement to the flies upon them.

The Basket or *Creel* should not be large and cumbersome, and should neatly fit the back.

The Landing-net should be light, the handle long, and the net deep.

Nothing need here be said of the usual and very necessary *Clearing-ring*, or of a few other little necessaries, conveniences, and luxuries, which tackle-makers know so well how to describe and recommend. These gentlemen should be listened to, even although one may sometimes pay rather dearly for the whistle. More fish than cash is taken by their nets after all; and every body knows the peculiar comfort of being well provided with tackle (and *Prog* by the by) when distant from the sources of provision. We also know the pride and pleasure of supplying a "Venator" with a seasonable well-made fly or a length of gut, &c.

RECIPES FOR DYEING AND STAINING FEATHERS, ETC.

1. TO DYE WHITE FEATHERS A DUN COLOUR.

Make a mordant by dissolving about a quarter of an ounce of alum in a pint of water, and slightly boil the feathers in it, taking care that they shall be thoroughly soaked or saturated with the solution, then boil them in other water with fustick, shumach, and a small quantity of copperas, put into it until they have assumed the required tint. The fustick and copperas will make a yellow dun tint; the shumack and copperas a blue dun tint. The greater the quantity of copperas the deeper will be the dye.

2. TO TURN RED HACKLES BROWN.

Put a piece of copperas the size of half a walnut into a pint of water; boil it, and whilst boiling put in the red feathers. Let them remain until by frequent examination they are found to have taken the proper colour.

3. TO STAIN FEATHERS AN OLIVE DUN, ETC.

Make a very strong infusion of the outside brown leaves or coating of an onion root, by allowing the ingredients to stand warm by the fire for ten or twelve hours. If dun feathers are boiled in this dye they will become an olive dun; and white feathers a yellow. If a small piece of copperas be added the latter colour will become a useful muddy yellow, darker or lighter as may be required, and approaching to a yellow olive dun, according to the quantity of copperas used.

4. TO DYE A MALLARD'S FEATHER FOR THE GREEN DRAKE.

Tie up some of the best feathers in bunches of a dozen, and boil them in the same mordant of alum as given in No. 1, merely to get the grease out. Then boil them in an infusion of fustick to procure a yellow, and subdue the brightness of this yellow by adding copperas to the infusion.

5. TO DYE FEATHERS DARK RED AND PURPLE.

Hackles of various colours boiled (without alum) in an infusion of logwood and Brazil wood dust, until they are as red as they can be made by this means, may be changed to a deeper red by putting them into a mixture of muriatic acid and tin, and to a purple by a warm solution of potash. As the muriatic acid is not to be *saturated* with tin, the solution must be much diluted. If it burns your tongue much, it will burn the feathers a little.

6. TO DYE FEATHERS VARIOUS SHADES OF RED, AMBER, AND BROWN.

First boil them in the alum mordant (see No. 1); secondly, boil them in an infusion of fustick strong enough to bring them to a bright yellow (about a table spoonfull to a pint of water), then boil them in a dye of mather, peach wood, or Brazil wood. To set the colour, put a few drops of "*dyers spirit*," (i. e. nitrate of tin combined with a small quantity of common salt,) which may be had from a silk dyer, into the last mentioned dye.

7. TO STAIN SILK GUT THE COLOUR OF RET, WEEDS, ETC.

Make an infusion of onion coatings (see No. 3), put the gut into it when *quite cold*, and let it remain until the hue becomes as dark as may be required.

Gut may be stained in an infusion of green tea, a useful colour for some waters.

A dye of logwood will turn it to a pale blue.

Chapter III.

MANNER OF FISHING FOR TROUT AND GRAYLING.

Preparation of the Rod and Line. Art of Throwing. Choice of Weather. State of the Water. Choice of a Fly. Appearance of Life to be given to the Fly. Buzz flies sometimes preferred. Rising short, &c. Sudden cessation of Rises, &c. Places to be whipped, &c. Throwing to a Trout just risen. Striking. Killing. Landing. Differences between Trout and Grayling-fishing. Manner of presenting the Fly to a Grayling. Landing, &c.

When the rod is put together the rings upon it should fall into a line with each other. The reel containing the line is sometimes fastened to a belt round the body, but generally attached to the rod at the distance of ten to fourteen inches from the end of the but, (i. e.) that place where it produces a small and pleasant degree of counterbalance to the upper end of the rod. The fine end of the line with a loop receives the foot line, and to the fine end of the foot line is attached a fly or palmer, which is called the Stretcher. Other flies, which are made fast to the foot line, are called Droppers, two of which are generally sufficient. The first dropper is placed at about one yard distant from the stretcher, the second about three quarters of a yard from the first, each upon a piece of gut about four inches long. And the knots used for this purpose are so contrived, that they can be detached and resumed at pleasure.

Throwing.

In order to acquire the art of throwing a fly, it may be advisable to practise, previously to visiting the stream, in an open space free from trees, where a piece of paper may represent the spot required to be thrown to. Taking the wind in his back, the tyro, with a short line at first, may attempt to cast within an inch or two of the paper, and afterwards by degrees lengthen his line as his improvement proceeds; he may then try to throw in such a direction that the wind may in some measure oppose the line and rod; and lastly, he may practise throwing against the wind. In this way any person may become an adept in throwing a fly, much sooner than by trusting solely to the experience which he may get when at the water-side; for his attention being then wholly engrossed by the hopes of a rise, &c. a bad habit may be very easily engendered, which will not be as easily got rid of.

He should endeavour to impart to the line a good uniform sweep or curve round the head; for if it returns too quickly or sharply from behind him, a crack will be heard and the fly whipped off. There is some little difficulty in acquiring this management. The larger the fly the more resistance it meets with in the air; this resistance causes it to make a better curve, and the danger of smacking it off is lessened. A Palmer made as shewn in plate 19 is not easily lost in this manner.

The attempt to describe by words *all* the precautions and manipulations requisite for throwing a fly successfully and gracefully would be as hopeless a task as that of teaching to dance by such means It must be abundantly evident that the fly should drop as lightly as possible on the water, and that an awkward unmannerly *splash* will inevitably mar the delusion.

Weather, &c.

The best days to select for fly fishing are those that are warm and cloudy, with a gentle breeze from the South or West, causing a ripple upon the water; by which the fish is not only prevented from seeing the fisherman so plainly as in smooth water, but is also deprived of so good an opportunity of detecting the fly-maker's artifice.

The water after a flood sometimes remains for several days too turbid for fly fishing. When it is very low in its bed and clear it is also unpropitious, and success is obtained with difficulty. When the water is unusually high, though it be *not* discoloured, the fish seem to be feeding more at the bottom than above: but these two last obstacles will not deter the sportsman from trying his skill.

Choice of Flies.

The selection of a fly requires more judgment, experience, and patience, than any other branch of the art. The beginner will soon discover that his choice cannot be absolutely decided by reference to the catalogue in the following chapter merely, or to any catalogue whatever. For when a fly is (in the former) said to be in season, it does not follow that it is abroad every day of its existence. The state of the weather, in respect of heat and moisture, have great influence in this respect; he should therefore bear in mind that the Coleoptera, or Beetle, will be on the water on hot days principally. The Ephemera, or fish fly, on rather cold days. The Phryganea, or water fly, as the Granam, &c. on cloudy days with gleams of sunshine. The Diptera and other land flies on windy days, as the Cow Dung, &c. He would often do well to begin fishing with a Palmer as a stretcher, and the fly which *seems* most suitable for the day as a dropper, one yard and three-quarters from it:

not changing these until he can discover what fly the fish are actually rising at. The Palmer is never totally out of season, and is *a good fat bait.*

It should never be forgotten, that, let the state of the weather or the water (in respect of clearness) be what it may, success in fly fishing very much depends upon shewing the fish a good imitation, both in colour and size, of that insect which he has recently taken: an exact resemblance of the shape does not seem to be quite so essential a requisite as that of colour, since the former varies, according to the position of the insect either in or upon the water; but a small fly is usually employed when the water is fine, because the fish is then better enabled to detect an imitation, and because the small fly is more easily imitated. The resemblance of each particular colour, &c. is not required to be so exact as in the case of a large fly.

When the fly is thrown on the stream, some little resemblance of life must be attempted to be given to it; this I imagine to be best accomplished by throwing across and down the current; the top of the rod should in this case, after throwing, be held over the side of the stream, on which the fisherman stands, ready to strike; the current will then act against the part of the line lying on the water, and cause the fly to sail over towards the same side, yet still to float down a little, as a natural fly when struggling might be supposed to do.

When the fly is thrown into a still place, a few gentle jerks (after it has remained a second or two on the water) may be given to it; but no greater force should be used than is sufficient to move it an inch or two at a time.

Some fishermen frequently prefer their flies made buzz, (i. e.) representing probably flies with their wings fluttering, or in rapid motion; whilst others succeed best with their flies made with the wings to represent the appropriate natural wings *at comparative rest.* Probably a difference in the mode of fishing may create this difference of choice in the make of a fly. He whose manner of fishing is that of throwing down the stream, close to the bank on which he stands, and then drawing the fly up the current, towards him, or in any manner giving it a good deal of motion, may find that the Buzz fly, made with a three year old cock's hackle, is best suited to that method, on account of the above mentioned fluttering appearance;* whilst

* Any person may become convinced of this resemblance by visiting the Serpentine in Hyde Park (or similar waters) on a warm evening of April, and by very carefully watching the motions of the Golden Dun (see Chap. IV. No. 10) immediately after it has quitted its nympha state. He will then see it *buzzing* along upon the surface of the water for some yards (previously to taking flight) and assuming an appearance exactly like that of the buzz-hackle, &c.

the artificial wings, resembling the natural wings of a fly partially immersed in the water, would be more suitable to the quieter mode of fishing.

Much valuable time is frequently lost by changing the fly often. It is better to persevere with that which produces tolerable sport, than to do so.

Rising short, &c.

A fish is said to *rise short* when he does not seize the bait voraciously and confidently, and this want of zeal is no doubt frequently occasioned by the imitation shewn to him being a too faint resemblance of the real insect.

Fish will sometimes rise freely at one moment, and in ten minutes afterwards not a rise is to be seen. *One* frequent cause of this is no doubt a want of food to rise at. A sudden change of weather, so slight as to be hardly perceptible to us, may have great influence upon the insects, as we perceive that it often has upon cows, asses, dogs, and many other animals.

Another cause for diminution or total loss of sport may be the falling of the water in the bed of the brook or river, occasioned by the stopping of a mill above the situation of the fisherman. I have observed from the fishing-house very frequently a remarkable diminution of rises in a given interval, to occur as soon as the water began to drop in consequence of such a stoppage. When this case occurs he will, generally, do better by going below the next mill which is working, or above that which has just stopped, than by remaining in the first place.

We have already pointed out in the plan or map, and in (Chap I. p. 4) the places in a brook where Trout and Grayling are chiefly to be found: such places should be carefully whipped. Two or three throws in the same place is generally sufficient.

We have also shewn (Chap. I. p. 8) the advantage of avoiding high stations, of seeking low ones, of stooping down sometimes as low as possible, and even of wading, (provided that the man takes care not to get " caught by the fish.") Water-proof fishing boots as used in Scotland are good things.

The precaution of preventing our shadow, and even that of the rod from falling on the water, should also be adopted.

Throwing to a Fish just risen and killing him.

When a fish has just risen at a natural object, it is well for the fisherman to try to throw into the curl occasioned by the rise, and left as a mark for him, but should the undulations have nearly died away, before he can throw to the spot, then he should throw, as nearly as he can judge, a yard or two above it, and allow the flies to float down to the supposed place of the fish; if a rise does not occur, it may be concluded that the fish has removed without seeing the flies; he may then try a yard or two on each side of the place where the curl appeared, when he may probably have a rise, and may possibly hook the fish, provided he has the knack of striking, which knack, like all others, is acquired only by practice; it must be done by a very sudden but not a very strong stroke, a twitch of thé wrist. Having hooked him, the rod should be carefully retained in that position which will allow its greatest pliability to be exerted. (For beginners to do this, it may be advisable that they should get it up over the shoulder, and present the but end towards the fish.) A gentle pull must now be kept upon the fish, and he should be led down the stream rather than up, (making use of the reel as occasion may require to shorten the line.) But if he runs in towards the bank upon which the fisherman stands, it will be necessary for him to approach the edge of the water as nearly as possible, holding the rod with an outstretched arm in almost an horizontal position, and if the reel is of the usual bad construction, it will be also necessary to pull in the line as quickly as possible with the left hand, this may prevent the fish from reaching his harbour: if it should not, he will most likely twist the gut round roots, &c. and break away.

To kill him, the nose must be kept up as much as possible; should he be very importunate and resolute, he may be lent a little more line now and then, but it must be promptly retaken with tremendous interest, and got up as short as possible. After various fruitless efforts to escape, which exhausts his strength, the nose may be got fairly out of the water, he may be towed gently to the side, and the landing net passed under him.

From the time of hooking the fish, if a large one, to the time of landing, care must be had that the line shall not be touched by the hand, excepting under the just mentioned circumstances; all should depend upon the pliability of the rod. In case a landing net should not be at hand, the reel may be stopped from running back, the rod stuck up in the ground by the spike, and both hands being disengaged, the fisherman may stoop down and grasp him firmly behind the gills.

If a fish of less than half a pound is hooked fairly, he may be cautiously lifted out by the line, but should he begin to struggle in the least degree, he must be allowed to drop into the water, where he will be again under the influence of the pliable rod, when he must be towed up again and another effort made to secure him.

The principal differences between Trout and Grayling Fishing are, that the latter requires a more delicate hand, a quicker eye, and the use of smaller flies upon the finest gut. The strike must be made on the instant of the rise. The fish may be sometimes seen, if he be of a good size and the water bright, a few inches before he gets up to the fly, and the fisherman must strike immediately that he does so, for his motion at the instant of seizure is too rapid to be visible.

When the fisherman comes upon a favourable place for Grayling, he should recollect that this fish does not follow the fly as the Trout does, and should therefore allow it to float down the stream in a natural way; for should a Grayling be waiting for it, and it is drawn away, " the fish will be disappointed of that which it was the fisherman's intention to entertain him with."

It must also be remarked here that the mouth of the Grayling is much more tender than that of the Trout, therefore much more care in landing is required; and a landing net is generally indispensable, especially where the banks are high, for the mouth will seldom bear his weight out of the water.

Chapter IV.

OF A SELECTION OF INSECTS, AND THEIR IMITATIONS, USED IN FLY FISHING.

Flies, &c. used in March. Flies, &c. for April. For May. For June. For July. For August. For September. Palmers for the Season.

It would much exceed the proper limits and purpose of a Fishing Book to enter upon the details by which even the Genera and Orders, to which every fly here spoken of belongs, are known to the Entomologist. Reference can easily be made. by means of the names placed on the pages opposite to the plates, to sources of abundant information on these points; but the names of some species and varieties of Ephemera mentioned, would in vain be sought for.

All the vulgar names known to me of each insect are given for the purpose of assisting fishermen of various counties to recognize it. And the order in which they are placed, is that of the months in which they are used, as forming, perhaps, the most convenient arrangement for his purposes.

The term Dun appears to have been applied in a *general* sense to the different species of Ephemeridæ, in their first winged state, (except those of the largest size,) another term being added to designate *each* species, as the *Blue* Dun, *Yellow* Dun, &c.

In like manner the term Spinner seems to have been applied as a *general* name for the final change or perfect state of the same insects, another name also being added to distinguish *each* species, as the *Red* Spinner, *Great Red* Spinner, &c.

It may be here added, that the Imitations of the Palmers are, to the best of my knowledge and belief, new; and I beg leave to assure my brother Anglers, that they have proved very effective. The figures represent the insect in its medium size; it may be made and used either larger or smaller.

It should also be stated that the length of the lives of the Ephemeridæ described below, is estimated by the time they lived in boxes.

No. 1. RED FLY.

Order, Neuroptera.
Family, Perlidæ.
Genus, Nemoura.

No. 2. COCK WING. (BLUE DUN, COCK TAIL.)

Order, Neuroptera.
Family, Ephemeridæ.
Genus, Baetis.

No. 3. RED SPINNER.

Order, Neuroptera.
Family, Ephemeridæ.
Genus, Baetis.

Pl. IV

No. 1. RED FLY.

In a forward spring this fly comes out about the middle of February, it is in season until the end of March, and may be used on fine but rather windy days, until the Blue Dun (see No. 2) and other flies come in. I have taken very large Grayling with it.

IMITATION.

BODY. The dubbing is composed of the dark red part of squirrel's fur, mixed with an equal quantity of claret-coloured mohair, shewing the most claret colour at the tail of the fly. This is spun on, and warped with brown silk thread.

WINGS. From a ginger dun covert feather of the mallard's wing. The pea hen has also feathers of the exact tint.

LEGS. Of a claret-coloured *stained* hackle. No feather of its *natural* colour, that I know of, is of the proper shade.

To make it buzz, a copper tinged dun hackle is wound upon the above body.

No. 2. COCK WING.

This fly lives three or four days in the state represented; then becomes the Red Spinner, (see No. 3.) It begins to be plentiful in the early part of March, or a little sooner, should the weather be mild. When in full season it will be found on the water, chiefly on rather cold windy days. It endeavours to take flight in three or four seconds after it leaves its Nympha. On cold days it seems to have rather more difficulty in rising from the water than in warm weather, and consequently becomes very frequently food for fishes at the moment of its new birth.

IMITATION.

Body. Fur of a hare's ear, or face, spun on yellow silk. When this dubbing-spun silk is warped on, some of the longest part of the dubbing is left out to form legs.

Tail. Two small whiskers of a rabbit.

Wings. From a feather of the starling's wing, slightly stained in onion dye, (see List of Dyes.)

Legs. If a sufficient quantity of dubbing was not left out for the legs, whilst the body was made, more must be picked out of it with a needle.

No. 3. RED SPINNER.

This is the name given to the Blue Dun (see No. 2.) after it has cast off its olive brown coat. It now appears of a bright red brown, and its wings, which were before rather opaque, are transparent. It lives four or five days. It sports in the sunshine, and will be more successfully used in warm than cold weather; but when the sun becomes too powerful, this delicate insect seems to be disabled from continuing abroad in the middle of the day, and is to be considered more as an evening fly. Several of the other spinners (or perfect Ephemeridæ) resemble it so nearly, that it may be kept as a model; the tint only varying, (as will be subsequently shewn).

IMITATION.

BODY. Brown silk, ribbed with fine gold twist.

TAIL. Two whisks of a red cock's hackle.

WINGS. From a mottled grey feather of the mallard, stained to match the colour of the natural wings.

LEGS. Plain red cock's hackle.

No. 4. WATER CRICKET.

Order, Hemiptera.
Family, Hydrometridæ.
Genus, Velia.
Species, Currens.

No. 5. GREAT DARK DRONE. (SAW FLY, GREAT DARK DUN.)

Order, Hymenoptera.
Family, Tenthredinidæ.
Genus, Dolerus.

No. 6. COW DUNG FLY.

Order, Diptera.
Family, Muscidæ.
Genus, Scatophaga.
Species, Stercoraria.

Pl I

4

5

4

5

No. 4. WATER CRICKET.

This insect lives upon small flies, &c. whose blood it sucks in a manner similar to that of the land spider. It runs upon the water, and darts upon its prey whilst struggling on the surface, and is one amongst the first insects which the Trout finds there. In the hot summer months it is provided with wings. It may be fished with throughout this month, and the next, on all sorts of days, but principally when the Blue Dun is *not* very abundant upon the water.

IMITATION.

BODY. Orange floss silk, tied on with black silk thread.

LEGS. Are made best of one of the two longest feathers of a peawit's topping. If this cannot be easily procured, a black cock's hackle will answer the purpose. Either of these must be wound all down the body, and the fibres then *snipped* off, as far up as is shewn in the figure.

No. 5. GREAT DARK DRONE.

This fly is found upon the grass in a *very dull* (almost torpid) state, until nine or ten o'clock in the morning; (whence its name of Drone) but when the sun begins to warm the air, it takes wing; and afterwards, if there be a slight breeze, it will be found upon the water.

There is a great variety of colour in the family. A bright orange is sometimes seen all over the body, a lemon colour sometimes pervades only the middle part of the body, the knee joints are sometimes tipped with orange, sometimes orange veins appear in the wings; but the black body is by far the most frequently met with, and therefore the fly with this colour is usually fished with.

IMITATION.

Body. Mole fur, or black ostrich feather, warped with black silk.

Wings and Legs. Made buzz with a dun hackle, the tint lighter than that of the natural wings. (See Chap. II. p. 31.)

When this fly is made with wings and legs not buzz, the dun feather of the wing of the mallard is used, and a grizzle hackle for legs, upon the same body.

No. 6. COW DUNG FLY.

This fly is to be seen throughout the year. In the young state it is very abundant about the middle of March, when vast quantities are seen upon the water if there be a high wind. The colour of the male, when newly hatched, is a very bright tawny yellow, that of the female a greenish brown; she is rather smaller than the male, is found in as great numbers on the water, and is as good a fly to imitate. This insect is not in full season after the end of April, but in very blustering days may be used all the year round.

IMITATION.

Body. Yellow worsted, mohair, or camlet, mixed with a little dingy brown fur from the bear, and left rather rough, spun upon light brown silk.

Wings. From the landrail.

Legs. Of a ginger coloured hackle.

The female is made buzz thus:

Body. Olive-coloured mohair, or worsted, spun on silk of the same colour.

Wings and Legs. Of a red cock's hackle, changed to a brown colour by putting it into a solution of copperas. (See Dyes, Chap. II. p. 33, article 2).

No. 7. PEACOCK FLY.

Order, *Coleoptera*.
Family, *Staphylinidæ*.
Genus, *Lathrobium*.
Species, *Elongatum*.

No. 8. MARCH BROWN. (DUN DRAKE, called in Wales the COB FLY.)

Order, *Neuroptera*.
Family, *Ephemeridæ*.
Genus, *Baetis*.

No. 9. GREAT RED SPINNER, (or LIGHT MACKEREL.)

Order, *Neuroptera*.
Family, *Ephemeridæ*.
Genus, *Bäetis*.

No. 7. PEACOCK FLY.

This small beetle is extremely abundant on warm sunny days. Its usual habit on alighting is to gather up the wings under its short wing scales, (a habit like that of the earwig, which flies about in Autumn); but when it falls upon water, it cannot always succeed in doing so; then therefore the wings lie nearly flat upon its back. However fine the day may be, and however clear the water, some sport may still be expected with this fly, until the end of May, but it is most successfully used on a sultry gloomy day.

IMITATION.

BODY. Brown peacock's herl, dressed with mulberry-coloured silk.

WINGS. The darkest part of a wing feather of the starling.

LEGS. A hackle stained dark purple; appearing black when looked down upon; but when held up to the light, having a most beautiful dark tortoiseshell hue. (See Dyes, Chap. II. p. 34, article 5).

No. 8. MARCH BROWN.

The pupa or nympha of this fly seems to require a warmer day to enable it to rise to the surface of the water, and to change to a fly, than is required for the similar rise and metamorphosis of the Blue Dun's nympha (No. 2); the fly lives three days in the state represented in the figure, then changes into the Great Red Spinner, (see fig. 9). The male has a chocolate hue, and the female a green brown; it generally appears in great numbers upon the streams, where it is found towards the latter end of March, and is very eagerly devoured by the Trout. It continues in season until May; and although it may occasionally be found later, I do not recommend the use of it after that time.

IMITATION.

Body. Fur of the hare's face ribbed over with olive silk, and tied with brown.

Tail. Two stands of a partridge feather.

Wings. Feather of the pheasant's wing, which may be found of the exact shade.

Legs. A feather from the back of a partridge.

No. 9. GREAT RED SPINNER.

The Dun Drake (fig. 8.) changes into this spinner, and enjoys for three or four days its newest state and title. It seems to be in season much longer than the Dun Drake, and may even be used on warm evenings during most of the summer months; yet although the Dun Drake is not seen on the water after the middle of May, it would seem that it must still continue to come into existence afterwards, otherwise the Great Red Spinner could be in season only three or four days longer than the Dun Drake.*

IMITATION.

Body. Hog's down dyed red-brown, (or orange and brown floss silk mixed), spun on brown silk. It is ribbed with fine gold twist.

Tail. Two long whisks of a bright amber red stained hackle.

Wings. From a feather of the starling's wing.

Legs A bright amber red stained hackle.

* Although I have spoken of this Spinner as appearing throughout most of the summer months, I am by no means certain that the individuals which are produced later than the middle of May, may not be a distinct although very similar species of Baetis.

No. 10. GOLDEN DUN MIDGE.

Order, *Diptera.*
Family, *Tipulidæ.*
Genus, *Chironomus.*
Species, *Plumosus.*

No. 11. SAND FLY.

Order, *Trichoptera.*
Family, *Phryganidæ*
Genus, *Phryganea.*

No. 12. STONE FLY.

Order, *Neuroptera.*
Family, *Perlidæ.*
Genus, *Perla*
Species, *Bicaudata.*

Pl. VII

No. 10. GOLDEN DUN MIDGE.

The male has two feathered horns which the female has not. It seems to require a warm day to disengage itself from its water nympha. On such days very great sport may be had with it until the end of May.

IMITATION.

BODY. Olive floss silk ribbed with gold twist, and tied with dun silk thread.

WINGS. From the palest feather of a young starling.

LEGS. A plain dun hackle.

No. 11. SAND FLY.

This fly comes from a water larva. It is highly extolled by Mr. Bainbridge, who says, "that it may be reckoned as one of the best flies for affording diversion which can possibly be selected, for it may be used successfully at all hours of the day, from April to the end of September, and is equally alluring to the Trout and Grayling." (Fly Fisher's Guide, p. 143). My own experience leads me to recommend the use of it during April and May, on days when there is no abundance of any particular insect on the water. A fly very like it is used in September and October, called the Cinnamon Fly.

IMITATION.

BODY. Of the sandy coloured fur from the hare's neck, spun on silk of the same colour.

WINGS. From the landrail's wing made full.

LEGS. From a light ginger feather from the neck of a hen.

This fly is made buzz with a feather from the underside of the wing of the throstle, wound upon the above body.

No. 12. STONE FLY.

This fly comes from a water larva. It is heavy in its flight, but uses its legs with extreme activity, and is generally found amongst the stones, or close to the sides of the water. I have kept an individual alive for three weeks, during which time it drank much water. It is in season from the beginning of April until the end of May, and should be used in the rapid parts of streams, and on windy days where the water is rough.

IMITATION.

BODY. Fur of hare's ear mixed with yellow worsted or camlet, ribbed over with yellow silk, leaving most yellow at the tail.

TAIL. A mottled stand or two of a partridge feather.

WINGS. Feather from the pheasant's wing.

LEGS. A hackle stained greenish-brown.

HORNS. Two rabbit's whiskers.

No. 13. GRAVEL BED. (SPIDER FLY.)

Order, Diptera
Family, Tipulidæ.
Genus, Anisomera.
Species, Obscura.

No. 14. GRANNOM. (GREEN TAIL.)

Order, Trichoptera.
Family, Phryganidæ.
Genus, Tinodes.

No 15. YELLOW DUN.

Order, Neuroptera.
Family, Ephemeridæ.
Genus, Baetis.

Pl. VIII

No. 13. GRAVEL BED.

This fly is not upon all waters: upon those where it is found it is extremely numerous on fine days; but in cold weather it seeks shelter amongst the larger stones of the gravel. It may be used all the day. It comes in about the middle of April and lasts about three weeks.

IMITATION.

BODY. Dark dun, or lead-coloured silk thread dressed very fine.

WINGS. From the underside of a feather of the woodcock's wing.

LEGS. A black cock's hackle rather long, wound twice, only, round the body.

To make it buzz, a dark dun cock's hackle tinged brown may be used.

No. 14. GRANNOM.

This fly comes from a water larva, and is upon the surface at about the same season as the Gravel Bed, (No. 13), and chiefly in the morning and evening. It lasts a little longer. The green tint of its body is derived from the colour of the eggs. It lays these upon the water. There are several varieties, but the figure (14) represents the most common kind, and I have taken many of these flies out of the stomachs of Trout, even in August, which had a green colour at the tail of their bodies, and were as nearly as possible of the same size and general tint as those of April.

IMITATION.

BODY. Fur of hare's face left rough, spun on brown silk. A little green floss silk may be worked in at the tail to represent the bunch of eggs there.

WINGS. Feather from the partridge's wing, and made very full.

LEGS. A pale ginger hen's hackle.

Made buzz with a feather from the back of the partridge's neck, wound upon the above body.

No. 15. YELLOW DUN.

This fly proceeding from a water nympha, lives in the form shewn about three days. It is on the water generally from ten o'clock until three, and is one of our best.

IMITATION.

BODY. Yellow mohair, mixed with a little pale blue fur from a mouse. Or yellow silk thread well waxed with cobbler's wax to give it an olive tint.

WINGS. The lightest part of a feather from a young starling's wing.

LEGS. A light yellow dun hackle.

To make it buzz, a lighter dun hackle than is represented in the figure, is wound upon the same body.

This Yellow Dun changes to a Spinner of rather a lighter and yellower brown, than that which the Blue Dun (No. 2) turns to, is very nearly of the same size, and lives nine days. It is to be used on warm evenings. Its imitation may consequently be made of the same materials as that of the Red Spinner, (see No. 3), only choosing lighter tints.

No. 16. IRON BLUE DUN.

Order, *Neuroptera.*
Family, *Ephemeridæ.*
Genus, *Baetis.*

No. 17. JENNY SPINNER. (SPINNING JENNY.)

Order, *Neuroptera.*
Family, *Ephemeridæ.*
Genus, *Bäetis.*

No. 18. HAWTHORN FLY.

Order, *Diptera.*
Family, *Tipulidæ.*
Genus, *Bibio.*
Species, *Marci.*

Pl IX.

No. 16. IRON BLUE DUN.

After emerging from its water nympha, this fly remains about two days in the state shewn, and then changes to the Jenny Spinner, (see No. 17). It is one of the smallest flies worth the Angler's notice, but not the least useful. The male has a brownish red crown or cap on his head. The female is also crowned, but her cap is too small to be easily seen. It is in season from the latter end of April until the middle of June, and is on the water chiefly on cold days; influenced by effects similar to those which act upon the Blue Dun, (see No. 2).

IMITATION.

BODY. Blue fur from a mole. Reddish brown floss silk may be tied on for the head.

TAIL. A whisk or two out of a yellow dun hackle.

WINGS. From a feather of the under side of the cormorant's wing; or in default thereof, a feather from the breast of the water hen; the tip of which must be used. Or the upper end of the wing feather of a tomtit when in full plumage.

LEGS. A very small yellow dun hackle.

It is difficult to find a hackle feather of the tint proper to make this fly buzz.

No. 17. JENNY SPINNER.

This is the name given to the Iron Blue (No. 16) in his new dress, and it lives four or five days after the metamorphosis, sporting in the still summer atmosphere. The Iron Blue must be coming out of its nympha at the same time that this fly is in season; the Iron Blue is however found on the water chiefly on cold days, from the end of April until the middle of June.* The Jenny Spinner lasts all the Summer, is out on mild days, particularly towards the evening, and is a killing fly even when the water is extremely fine.

IMITATION.

BODY. White floss silk wound round the shank of the hook, &c. and tied on at the head and tail with brown silk, which must be shewn.

TAIL. A whisk or two of a light dun hackle.

WINGS AND LEGS Are best imitated by making them buzz; for which purpose the lightest dun hackle that can be procured should be used.

---

* A little dark dun with a brown head, not exactly similar to, but very much like the Iron Blue, is found in August, and then a Spinner like the Jenny Spinner, has an orange-coloured head, and the extremity of its body a lighter colour.

No. 18. HAWTHORN FLY.

This fly is by some called the black caterpillar. It has good wings, and makes good use of them. It may be seen about the last week in April, when the air is warm, sporting up and down by the sides of hedges, and may then be used. There are three very common species, one of the size represented, another much larger, and another much smaller. The female of each has dark wings, (almost black); whereas those of the male are a very pale blue, (almost white). Her head is very much smaller than that of the male, and her body thicker. The male is most abundant. The figure (18) represents him.

IMITATION.

Body. Black ostrich herl.
Wings. From a feather of the sea swallow.
Legs. A black cock's hackle; or one of the two largest feathers from a peawit's top-knot.

The fly cannot very easily be made buzz, unless the female is imitated, in which case a black hackle wound over the above mentioned black ostrich herl will answer the purpose.

No. 19. LITTLE YELLOW MAY DUN.

Order, Neuroptera.
Family, Ephemeridæ.
Genus, Bäetis.

No. 20. BLACK GNAT.

Order, Diptera.
Family, Empidæ.
Genus, Ramphamyia.

No. 21. DOWNHILL FLY. (Oak Fly, Ash Fly, Cannon Fly, Downlooker, Woodcock Fly, Downhead Fly.)

Order, Diptera.
Family, Rhagionidæ.
Genus, Rhagio.
Species, Scolopaceus.

Pl X

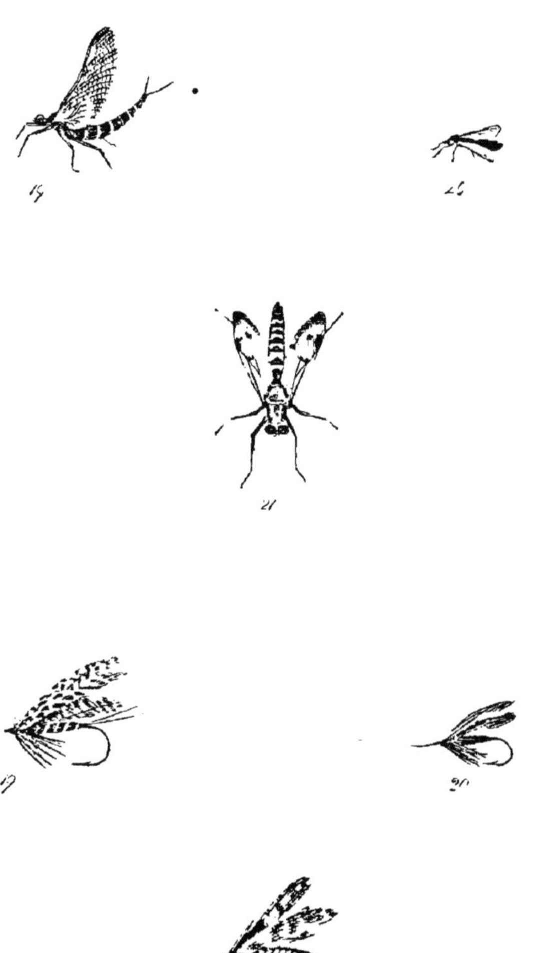

No. 19. LITTLE YELLOW MAY DUN.

This fly proceeding from a water nympha, remains in the state represented about three days, then changes to a very light red, or amber-coloured, spinner. It lasts (as shewn) in season until the Green Drake (No. 28) comes in at the end of May, or beginning of June.

IMITATION.

BODY. Pale ginger-coloured fur from behind the hare's ear, ribbed over with yellow silk thread.

TAIL. One or two whisks from a dun hackle.

WINGS. Mottled feather from the mallard, stained olive. (See list of Dyes, Chap. III. p. 34, article 4.)

LEGS. A light dun hackle also very slightly stained yellowish in the same dye.

The Light Amber Spinner, to which this fly changes, lives in its new state about four days. It is used successfully on the evenings of warm days.

No. 20. BLACK GNAT.*

This insect skims the brook all the day long in immense crowds, flying at great speed for about ten yards up and down the stream. When night approaches, or on cold wet days, it may be found on the grass at the water side. The stomachs of Trout have been found nearly gorged with this fly. It is in season from the beginning of May until the end of June.

IMITATION.

Body. Black ostrich herl.
Wings. The dark part of a feather from the starling.
Legs. A black hackle.

To make it buzz, a light dun hackle tinged with brown may be wound upon the above body.

---

* This is not a Gnat, although commonly called one by fishermen.

No. 21. DOWNHILL FLY.

This fly may be found upon the trunks of any kind of tree or post near the water side. As soon as it alights, it turns its head downward. It is in season throughout May and June, and may be used with most success on windy days.

IMITATION.

BODY. Orange floss silk tied with ash-coloured silk thread, which may be shewn at the tail and shoulders.

WINGS. From a feather of the woodcock.

LEGS. A furnace hackle, (i. e. a red cock's hackle, with a black list up the middle, and tinged with black also at the extremities of the fibres). This should be warped all down the body, and the fibres snipped off again nearly up to where the wings are set on, leaving a sufficient quantity for the legs uncut off.

No. 22. TURKEY BROWN, (LITTLE BROWN DUN.)

Order, Neuroptera
Family, Ephemeridæ.
Genus, Ephemera.

No. 23. LITTLE DARK SPINNER .

Order, Neuroptera.
Family, Ephemeridæ.
Genus, Ephemera

No. 24. YELLOW SALLY.

Order, Neuroptera.
Family, Perlidæ.
Genus, Perla.
Species, Lutea.

Pl XI

22

23

24

22

23

24

No. 22. TURKEY BROWN.

This fly comes from a water larva, lives two days as shewn, and then turns to the Little Dark Spinner, (see No. 23). It is to be used on cold days; is a very good fly upon some waters; and is in season from about the time that the March Brown becomes scarce until the end of June.

IMITATION.

BODY. Dark brown floss silk ribbed with purple silk thread.

TAIL. A whisk or two of a red cock's hackle, stained as for the legs.

WINGS. Tip of the brownest feather from a partridge's tail.

LEGS. Red cock's hackle stained a good brown with copperas.

To make it buzz, a feather from the Grouse may be tied on, in the manner shewn in the imitation of the Green Drake, No 28.

No. 23. LITTLE DARK SPINNER.

This is the metamorphosis of the Turkey Brown, (No. 22.) It is a most killing fly just at the beginning of dusk.

IMITATION.

Body. Mulberry-coloured floss silk ribbed over with purple silk thread.

Tail. Three or four whisks out of the stained hackle feather which is used for the legs.

Wings. From a feather of the starling's wing.

Legs. From a purple stained hackle which appears black when looked down upon, but which shines with a dark tortoiseshell tint, when held up between the eye and the light.

No. 24. YELLOW SALLY.

This fly comes from a water nympha. It has been believed by some persons to last in season only six days, but it continues for six weeks or more, and may be used not unprofitably on very hot days, when it is busily employed laying its eggs upon the water.

IMITATION.

BODY. Any yellowish buff fur ribbed with fawn coloured silk.

WINGS. From a wing feather of a white hen stained pale yellow.

LEGS. From an extremely pale ginger hackle, or a white feather dyed of a yellowish ginger tint.

No. 25. SKY BLUE.

Order, Neuroptera.
Family, Ephemeridæ.
Genus, Bäetis.

No. 26. FERN FLY (SOLDIER.)

Order, Coleoptera.
Family, Telephoridæ.
Genus, Telephorus.
Species, Livadus.

No. 27. ALDER FLY, (ORL FLY.)

Order, Neuroptera.
Family, Sialidæ.
Genus, Sialis.
Species, Niger.

Pl. XII

25

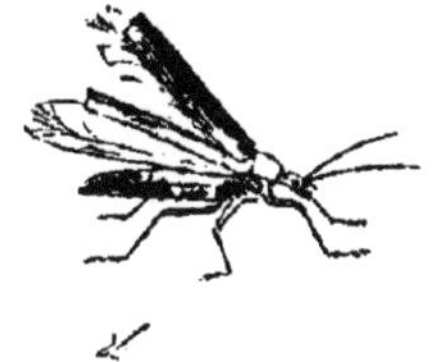

26

27

28

No. 25. SKY BLUE.

This fly comes from a water nympha, maintains its present state of existence two or three days, and then changes to a much lighter fly or spinner, which lives three or four days.

IMITATION.

BODY. Pale ginger mohair mixed with light blue fur.

TAIL. A whisk or two of the hackle used for the legs.

WINGS. From a feather of the sea swallow, or of a very light blue dun hen.

LEGS. Hackle stained a pale yellow

The body of the above mentioned spinner is more brilliant than that of the Sky Blue; the wings perfectly transparent, and almost colourless: it is very little used.

No. 26. FERN FLY.

Two of the most common varieties of this genus are known by the appellations of the soldier and the sailor, one wears a red the other a blue coat, both are much admired by fish, and taken until the end of July, principally on hot days. They live upon other insects, such as the aphides, or plant-lice.

IMITATION.

Body. Orange floss silk.
Wings. The darkest part of a feather from the starling's wing.
Legs. A red cock's hackle.

To make it buzz, a furnace-hackle (see p. 77) is wound upon the above body. It kills very well thus made.

No. 27. ALDER FLY.

This fly comes from a water nympha. It is earlier on some waters than on others. It lays its eggs upon the leaves of trees which overhang the water, and delights to skim the brook, but it may also be found at some distance from it. It is in season from about the last week in May until the end of June.

IMITATION.

Body. Dark mulberry floss silk, or peacock's herl, tied with black silk.
Wings. From a feather of a brown hen's wing.
Legs. Dark amber stained hackle, or in case of need a black cock's hackle will answer the purpose tolerably well.

To make it buzz, a dark dun hackle tinged brown may be wound upon the above body.

No. 28. GREEN DRAKE. (MAY FLY, CADOW.)

Order, Neuroptera.
Family, Ephemeridæ.
Genus, Ephemera.
Species, Vulgata.

No. 29. GREY DRAKE. (GLOSSY-WINGED DRAKE.)

Order, Neuroptera.
Family, Ephemeridæ.
Genus, Ephemera.
Species, Vulgata.

Pl XIII

No. 28. GREEN DRAKE.

This fly proceeding from a water nympha, lives three or four days as shewn; then the female changes to the Grey Drake, (No. 29) and the male to the Black Drake, (see p. 89). The Green Drake cannot be said to be in season quite three weeks on an average. Its season depends greatly upon the state of the weather; and it will be found earlier upon the slowly running parts of the stream, (such as mill dams) than on the rapid places.

IMITATION.

BODY. The middle part is of pale straw-coloured floss silk, ribbed with silver twist. The extremities are of a brown peacock's herl, tied with light brown silk thread.

TAIL. Three rabbit's whiskers.

WINGS AND LEGS. Made buzz from a mottled feather of the mallard, stained olive. (See Dyes, Chap. II. p. 35, article 4.)

To make it with wings in their state of rest, part of a feather similarly stained must be used, and a pale brown Bittern's hackle, or in case of need a partridge feather must be wrapped round the same body under the wings.

No. 29. GREY DRAKE.

This is the metamorphosis of the female Green Drake. She lives three or four days, and is caught by the fish whilst laying her eggs on the water. She lasts a few days longer than the Green Drake, and is to be fished with in the evening. Some fishermen prefer other flies in season to this; when well made, it will however furnish excellent sport, especially towards the evening. The buzz form is intended to imitate it when struggling and half drowned.

IMITATION.

BODY. The middle part is of white floss silk, ribbed over neatly with silver twist. The extremities are of a brown peacock's herl tied with brown silk thread.

TAIL. Three rabbit's whiskers.

WINGS AND LEGS. Made buzz from a mottled feather of the mallard, stained a faint purple.

To make it with wings at rest, the same pale purple stained feather may be used for them, and a dark purple stained hackle for the legs, upon the above body.

THE BLACK DRAKE

Is the male Green Drake metamorphosed. Its term of existence is about the same as that of the female above mentioned. It is smaller than the female, and very much darker, and is erroneously supposed by some, who call him the Death Drake, to kill her. He is never in season without her; but is not here represented because he is not so fat and tempting a bait.

No. 30. MARLOW BUZZ. (Hazel Fly, Coch-a-bonddu, Shorn Fly.)

Order, *Coleoptera.*
Family, *Chrysomelidæ.*
Genus, *Chrysomela.*
Species, *Populi.*

No. 31. DARK MACKEREL.

Order, *Neuroptera.*
Family, *Ephemeridæ.*
Genus, *Ephemera.*

Pl.

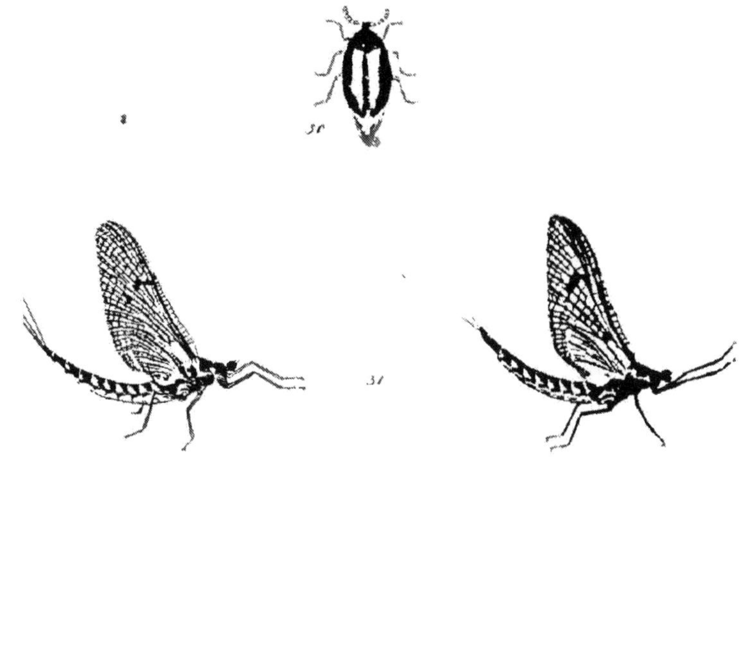

No. 30. MARLOW BUZZ.

This insect comes from a pupa which inhabits the earth. It is very abundant in hot weather at the water side, from the beginning until the middle of June, flying about amongst poplar trees, and feeding upon the leaves.

IMITATION.

BODY. Black ostrich herl twisted with peacock herl and black silk thread.

WINGS AND LEGS. Are made buzz with a dark furnace cock's hackle. (See p. 77.)

There are other varieties, some much smaller, of the Red Beetle, and Lady Bird, which may be imitated in a similar manner, and used when numerous. This is the largest ever employed.

To make it with wings at rest, the darkest part of the starling's wing, and a red cock's hackle may be wound upon the above body in the same way as for the Fern Fly, No. 26.

No. 31. DARK MACKEREL.

This is the name given to the insect represented by the figure on the right hand side of the plate, after it has changed from a dark kind of Green Drake shewn on the left side. Both the male and female change to the dark brown, but the former is the smallest and darkest fly. Their habits are similar in every respect to the Green and the Grey Drake, (Nos. 28 and 29). Sir H. Davy says, that "the Green Ephemera, or May Fly, lays her eggs sitting on the water." (Salmonia, p. 249.) My observations lead to the conviction that neither the dark nor light Green Ephemera lay eggs, (being imperfect insects,) but that their metamorphoses, the Grey Drake and the Dark Mackerel, lay eggs (whilst rising and falling, &c.)* This fly continues

* The egg of this fly and that of all the last metamorphoses of the Ephemeridæ, here spoken of, sinks to the bottom of the water, and is there, in a few days, hatched into a white grig; this larva undergoes several transmutations before it becomes a nympha, which, rising to the surface at its appointed season, bursts the case or skin which incloses it (at the shoulders), displays beautiful wings, quits its old husk, and, after the lapse of a second or two, generally flies to the nearest terra firma, where it remains in solitude and shelter (from the wind and sun-beams) for about two days, (see fig. 22, plate 11.) It then undergoes its last metamorphosis, and enters upon its imago or perfect state, (see fig. 23), changing the whole of its envelopes, even those of its fine tails and legs. The tails and the two fore legs of the male increase to about double

in season until the end of June, or for a few days in July.

IMITATION.

Body. Dark mulberry floss silk, ribbed with gold twist.

Tail. Three rabbit's whiskers.

Wings. From a brown mottled feather of the mallard, which hangs from the back over a part of the wing.

Legs. A purple dyed hackle, appearing black when looked down upon, but a dark tortoise-shell hue, when held between the eye and the light. (See Dyes, Chap. II. p. 35, article 5.)

---

their former length, those of the female receive an accession of not quite one third The colour is generally altered, the wings become shining and transparent. The male carries two large stemmata upon his head, and a pair of callipers at the end of his body, which two peculiarities chiefly distinguish his appearance from the female He is also usually rather smaller than she is. He may be seen merrily dancing, as it were, up and down in the air in vast crowds, frequently near a bush by the water side, whilst the female is to be discovered busily employed rising and falling and hovering over the water, and sometimes touching the surface and making use of her long tails to spring up again. She lays her eggs at this moment

The Larva and Nympha of the Genus Baetis have three tails, although the fly which comes immediately out of the Nympha has only two

No. 32. PALE EVENING DUN.

Order, *Neuroptera.*
Family, *Ephemeridæ.*
Genus, *Cloeon.*

No. 33. JULY DUN.

Order, *Neuroptera.*
Family, *Ephemeridæ.*
Genus, *Ephemera.*

No. 34. GOLD EYED GAUZE WING.

Order, *Neuroptera.*
Family, *Hemerobiidæ.*
Genus, *Hemerobius.*
Species, *Perla.*

Pl XV

32

33

34

32

'3

34

No. 32. PALE EVENING DUN.

This fly comes from a water nympha, lives two or three days as shewn, and then changes to a brighter yellow bodied fly. It may be strongly recommended as a fly which can be used when the water is fine.

IMITATION.

Body. Yellow martin's fur spun on pale fawn-coloured silk thread.

Wings. From a very fine grained feather of the starling's wing, stained of rather a lighter yellow than that which is used for the Green Drake, No. 28.

Legs. Pale dun hackle.

The brighter yellow bodied fly to which this changes lives four or five days, is fainter coloured, and more transparent in the wing. The change is not given, as the Dark Mackerel (No. 31) is very much preferable for the evening.

No. 33. JULY DUN.

This fly comes from a water nympha, lives three or four days as shewn, and then changes to a very small Dark Spinner. It affords a great treat to the Trout and Grayling, and lasts until the August Dun takes its place, in the beginning of August.

IMITATION.

Body. Mole's fur, and pale yellow mohair mixed and spun on yellow silk.

Tail. Two or three whisks of a dark dun hackle.

Wings. Dark part of a feather from the starling's wing, stained darker in strong onion dye.

Legs. Dark dun hackle.

To make it buzz, a lighter hackle may be wound upon the above body.

The tint of its metamorphosis is the same as that of the Dark Mackerel, No. 31. It will catch well late in the evening.

No. 34. GOLD EYED GAUZE WING.

This is rather a scarce insect upon some waters, but where it is found affords great sport on windy days. Both larger and smaller individuals than that represented, of this green sort, are to be found, and also a brown kind much larger and with dark round spots upon it. The eye possesses wonderful brilliancy. It may be used as soon as the Green Drake goes out, for about three weeks, (i. e.) towards the middle or end of this month.

IMITATION.

Body. Very pale yellowish green floss silk, tied on with silk thread of the same colour.

Wings and Legs. The palest blue dun hackle which can be procured.

No. 35. WREN TAIL. (Frog Hopper, Pale Brown Bent Hopper.)

Order, *Hemoptera*.
Family, *Cercopidæ*.
Genus, *Cercopis*.
Species, *Spumaria*.

No. 36. RED ANT.

Order, *Hymenoptera*.
Family, *Formicidæ*.
Genus, *Formica*.
Species, *Rufa*.

No. 37. SILVER HORNS. (Black Silver Twist.)

Order, *Trichoptera*.
Family, *Leptoceridæ*.
Genus, *Leptocerus*.

Pl XV

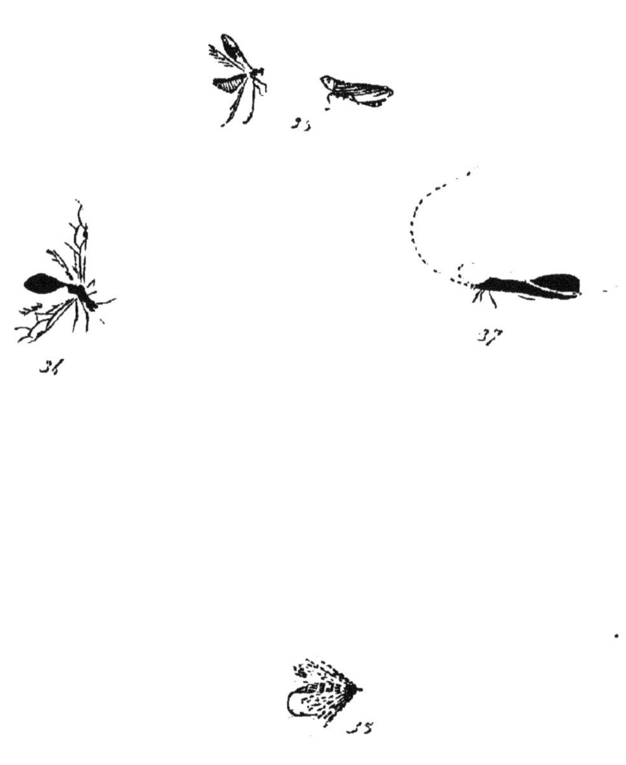

No. 35. WREN TAIL.

There are many varieties of this insect; the pale brown, the dark brown, and the greenish blue, are the most common. It is very busy on hot days hopping about and taking flights of about twenty yards, and this is the time to use it, for it sometimes drops short and falls upon the water. In colder weather it is found upon the long grass principally; not much on the water. On very cold days it seems to seek shelter near the roots of the grass.

IMITATION.

BODY. Ginger-coloured fur ribbed with gold twist.

WINGS AND LEGS. Feather from a wren's tail.

No. 36. RED ANT.

This insect is very abundant on the water after a swarm or flight of Ants and Emmets, the time of which is uncertain. There are two sorts; the black and the red of the size shewn, and two sorts much smaller which are used later in the season.

IMITATION.

Body. Peacock's herl tied with red-brown silk.
Wings. From a feather of the light part of a starling's wing.
Legs. A red cock's hackle.

The Black Ant is made of peacock's herl, and black ostrich mixed, for the body. Wings from the darkest part of the starling's wing, and legs a black cock's hackle.

No. 37. SILVER HORNS.

This fly is extremely abundant upon some waters, and is well taken both by the Trout and Grayling until the end of August throughout the day, and principally in showery weather. The figure represents the female. The male has black horns.

IMITATION.

Body. Black ostrich herl tied with black silk, and dressed off.

Wings. Feather from a wing of the cock blackbird.

Legs. Small black cock's hackle.

Horns. Grey feather of the mallard.

To make it buzz, the body is ribbed with silver twist upon the black ostrich herl, and a black hackle wrapt all down.

No. 38. AUGUST DUN.

Order, Neuroptera.
Family, Ephemeridæ.
Genus, Baetis.

No. 39. ORANGE FLY.

Order, Hymenoptera.
Family, Ichneumonidæ.
Genus, Cryptis

No. 40. CINNAMON FLY.

Order, Trichoptera.
Family, Phryganidæ.
Genus, Phryganea

Pl XVII

29

40

No. 38. AUGUST DUN.

This fly comes from a water nympha, lives two or three days as shewn, then changes to a Red Spinner. It is quite as important a fly for this month as the March Brown is for March. It is in season from the beginning of August to the middle of September.

IMITATION.

Body. Brown floss silk ribbed with yellow silk thread.

Tail. Two rabbit's whiskers.

Wings. Feather of a brown hen's wing.

Legs. Plain red hackle stained brown.

It is made buzz with a grouse feather wound upon the above body.

The Red Spinner, to which it changes, is very similar to that which the Blue Dun (No. 2) turns to, and is a good fly on a mild evening.

No. 39. ORANGE FLY.

This is one of the best flies that can be used both for Trout and Grayling. There are a great many varieties, some larger, some smaller than the representation. It may be used all day. Although discovered alive with difficulty, it is found abundant in the stomachs of the fish. It is furnished with an apparatus called the sting, used for the purpose of piercing the skin of caterpillars, in which it deposits its eggs, the grub from which grows in, and ultimately kills the insect in which it was hatched.

IMITATION.

BODY. Orange floss silk tied on with black silk thread.

WINGS. Dark part of the starling's wing, or feather of a hen blackbird.

LEGS. A very dark furnace hackle.

No. 40. CINNAMON FLY

This fly comes from a water pupa. There are many varieties. The larger variety being stronger can resist the force of rain and wind better than that represented, and are therefore not so well known to the fish. It should be used in a heavy shower, and also on a windy day. In both cases very great diversion may be expected with it.

IMITATION.

Body. Fawn-coloured floss silk, tied on with silk thread of the same colour.

Wings. Feather of a yellow brown hen's wing, rather darker than the landrail's wing feather.

Legs. A ginger hackle.

It is made buzz with a grouse feather or a red hackle stained brown with copperas, and tied on the same body.

No. 41. BLUE BOTTLE.

Order, Diptera.
Family, Muscidæ.
Genus, Musca.
Species, Vomitoria.

No. 42. WHIRLING BLUE DUN.

Order, Neuroptera.
Family, Ephemeridæ.
Genus, Baetis.

No. 43. LITTLE PALE BLUE DUN.

Order, Neuroptera.
Family, Ephemeridæ.
Genus, Cloeon.

No. 44. WILLOW FLY.

Order, Neuroptera.
Family, Perlidæ.
Genus, Nemoura.
Species, Nebulosa.

Pl. XVII

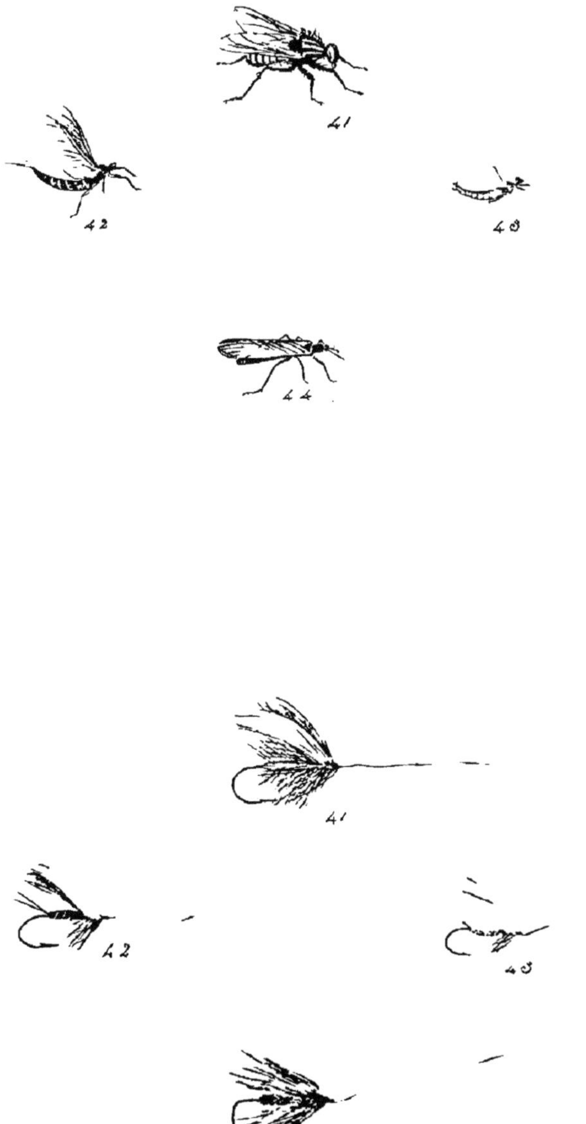

No. 41. BLUE BOTTLE.

This and the house fly become blind and weak in this month, and are therefore frequently driven on to the water on windy days, when very good sport may be expected with them. The Blue Bottle is perhaps to be preferred. It may be used until cold weather sets in.

IMITATION.

BODY. Bright blue floss silk tied with light brown silk thread, shewing the brown at the head.

WINGS. Feather of the starling's wing.

LEGS. Black hackle from a cock wrapped down the principal part of the body.

To make it buzz, a dark dun hackle may be wound upon the above body.

No. 42. WHIRLING BLUE DUN.

This fly comes from a water nympha, lives about three days as shewn, then turns to a Light Red Spinner. It is in season until the middle of October, and on the water chiefly in blustering cold weather. It has been supposed to be a second edition of the Yellow Dun of April. If compared with that it will be found rather smaller and more of a ginger-colour.

IMITATION.

BODY. Squirrel's red brown fur mixed with yellow mohair, tied with yellow silk thread well waxed.

TAIL. One or two whisks of a pale ginger hackle.

WINGS. Feather from a starling's wing not very light.

LEGS. Pale ginger hackle.

THE RED SPINNER lives three or four days. In making it, reference may be had to fig. 3, plate 4. It must be rather lighter than that figure.

No. 43. LITTLE PALE BLUE DUN.

This fly comes from a water nympha, lives two or three days as shewn, then changes to a more delicate fly than that represented. It is upon the water at the same time as the Whirling Blue, (No. 42) and lasts until the end of the fishing season. It is very abundant, and taken equally well by both Trout and Grayling.

IMITATION.

Body. Very pale blue fur mixed with a very little yellow mohair.

Wings. Feather from the sea swallow.

Legs. The palest blue hackle to be had.

To make it buzz, a sea swallow's feather only may be wound upon the same body.

The metamorphosis of this fly has very transparent wings. It is too delicate to be imitated.

No. 44. WILLOW (OR WITHY) FLY.

This fly comes from a water pupa. It is extremely abundant during this month and the next, and even later in the season. On very fine days it may even be found on the water in February. It generally flutters across the stream, and is best imitated buzz fashion.

IMITATION.

BODY. Mole's fur spun upon yellow silk.
WINGS AND LEGS. A dark dun cock's hackle strongly tinged a copper-colour.

Pl.

No. 45. RED PALMER.

This is the caterpillar of the Arctia caga or Tiger Moth. I have found this palmer more abundantly than any other early in the Spring, and can recommend use of it to be made as soon as the water is fit for fishing after a flood; also on windy days.

IMITATION.

Peacock herl with a red cock's hackle wrapped over it, and tied with dark brown silk thread.

No. 46. BROWN PALMER.

This is the caterpillar of the Spilosoma lubricepeda, or common Ermine Moth.

It will catch fish throughout the fishing season, and may be used with most success after a flood and on windy days.

IMITATION.

Mulberry-coloured worsted spun on brown silk thread, and a brown stained cock's hackle wrapped over the whole of it.

No. 47. BLACK PALMER.

This is the caterpillar of the Laciocampa rubi, or Fox Moth.

It is used at the same times as the Brown Palmer.

IMITATION.

Black ostrich herl ribbed with gold twist, and a red cock's hackle wrapped over it.

FINIS.

INDEX.

Lightning Source UK Ltd.
Milton Keynes UK
UKHW022315080223
416651UK00001B/119